The Essential Travel Guide for Unforgettable Destinations

Exploring Iconic Landmarks and Beyond in New York City

Contents

CHAPTER 1

Introduction

Photo by Joshua Earle from Unsplash

Hey there, fellow adventurers! Picture this: the streets of New York City, bustling with life, and in the midst of it all, meet Ethan, a wide-eyed explorer like you and me. He had always been intrigued by the enchanting allure of the Big Apple, and now, his dreams were about to come true.

As Ethan stepped onto the vibrant sidewalks of Manhattan, he couldn't help but feel a surge of excitement coursing through his veins. It was like stepping into a movie set, only it was real, and it was all his to explore.

Now, my friend, let me tell you what this book is about. We're here to be your trusty companions as you venture into the heart of New York City for an incredible adventure. Whether you're a first-timer or an old friend returning for more, we will show you the ropes, help you discover the best spots, and ensure you soak up every ounce of the city's magic.

And let me tell you. There's magic everywhere you turn. New York City has everything from iconic skyscrapers soaring into the sky to charming little corners tucked away in quiet neighborhoods. We want you to feel Ethan's excitement, that same sense of wonder as you uncover the city's hidden treasures and embrace the energy that pulses through its streets.

You see, New York City isn't just a place; it's a state of mind. It's the spirit of dreams coming to life, cultures colliding and harmonizing, and endless possibilities. It's a city that never sleeps because it's too busy dreaming big. And we're going to dive right into that dream together.

Get ready to be swept off your feet as we delve into the stories of iconic landmarks that have become symbols of the city's soul. From the awe-inspiring Statue of Liberty, welcoming all dreamers, to the dazzling lights of Times Square, New York City will leave you breathless with its charm. We'll take you through neighborhoods brimming with character, each with a story to share and mouthwatering delights to savor.

But before we get too excited, let's take a sneak peek at what's coming up in the chapters ahead. We will explore the nooks and crannies of this metropolis, uncovering its fascinating history and the legends that have shaped its identity. So buckle up, my friend, and prepare for a flowy adventure that will leave you feeling like a true New Yorker in no time!

Grab your favorite travel essentials, pack your curiosity, and let's hit the ground running. The charm of New York City awaits, and we will embrace it with open arms. Ready? Let's go!

CHAPTER 2

Practical Tips

Photo by Christopher Burns from Unsplash

Did you know that over 60 million adventurers, dreamers, and curious souls from all corners of the globe flock to New York City each year? Yes, you heard that right! This buzzing metropolis has become an irresistible magnet, attracting visitors like a moth to a flame. And guess what? You're about to join those ranks and experience the magic firsthand!

But hold on. Before you dive headfirst into the vibrant chaos of the Big Apple, we've got your back with some invaluable practical tips to make your journey smooth and seamless.

Trust us; navigating this city's craze can be both exhilarating and overwhelming, so a little insider knowledge goes a long way.

In this chapter, we'll equip you with all the necessary know-how to maximize your time and enjoyment in New York City. From mastering the art of the subway system (hint: it's like unlocking a secret passageway to the city's heart) to blending in with the locals (we'll help you go beyond looking like a tourist), we've got you covered!

Transportation

Transportation is crucial when traveling to New York due to its vast size and dense population. Efficient transportation options like subways, buses, and rideshare services enable easy access to iconic landmarks, diverse neighborhoods, and cultural attractions, ensuring a seamless and enjoyable travel experience.

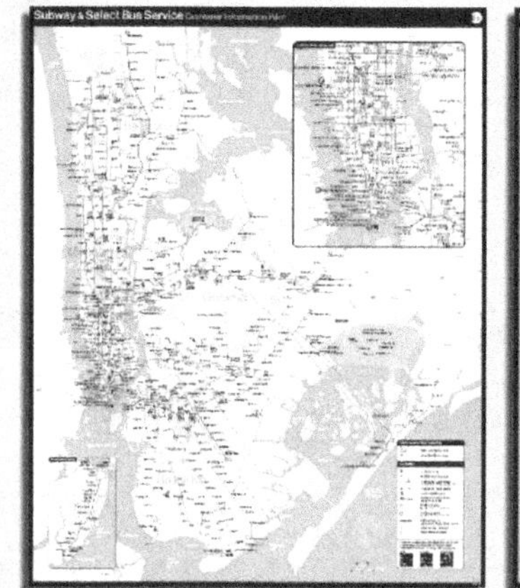

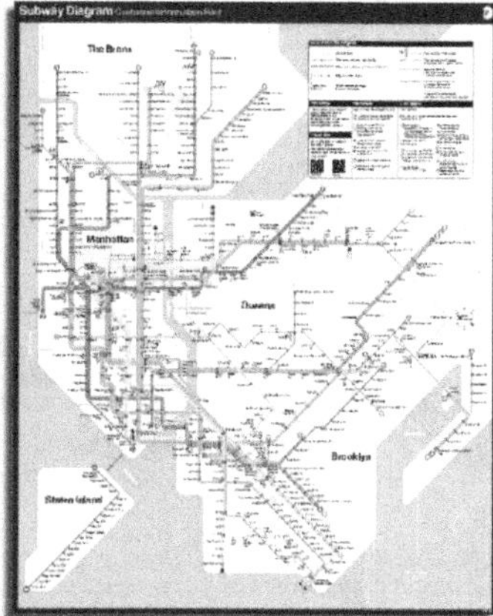

Photo by Fast Company

Getting In and Around the City

Airports:

- New York boasts multiple airports, including JFK, LaGuardia, and Newark Liberty, providing convenient entry points to explore the city's vibrant offerings.
- These airports are well-connected globally, making New York easily accessible from various parts of the world, ensuring a diverse and welcoming atmosphere for travelers.
- You can easily access taxis, rideshare services, and airport shuttles from the airports, allowing for a smooth transition to your accommodation or desired destinations.

- Look forward to modern amenities and services within the airports, such as shopping centers, dining options, and lounges, perfect for making your travel experience comfortable and enjoyable.
- To save time, consider using online check-ins and arriving early during peak travel, as these airports can get busy.

Public Transportation:

Photo by Ethan Hoover from Unsplash

- New York's public transportation system comprises an extensive network of buses and subways, linking every corner of the city, making it a cost-effective and efficient travel option.
- Invest in a MetroCard, the city's universal transit pass, which offers flexibility and ease when hopping on buses and subways without the need for cash transactions.
- Buses and subways run regularly throughout the day and night, reducing waiting times and allowing travelers to explore the city at their pace.
- Public transportation offers the chance to experience New York like a local, immersing yourself in its diverse neighborhoods, iconic landmarks, and lively atmosphere.

- Check MTA schedules and plan your routes using smartphone apps for real-time updates, ensuring a seamless and hassle-free journey.

Using Rideshare Services

Utilizing Rideshare Apps

- Rideshare apps offer a simple and intuitive interface, making it easy for users to request rides, select destinations, and track their drivers in real time.
- Enjoy the convenience of cashless payments through the app, as your fare is automatically charged to your linked payment method, eliminating the need for physical cash.
- Explore various ride-sharing options, such as carpooling, shared rides, or larger vehicles, to split costs with fellow travelers or reduce expenses on solo trips.
- Plan by scheduling rides in advance, especially for early morning or late-night travel, ensuring a reliable and prompt pick-up when needed.
- Rideshare apps allow passengers to rate drivers and provide feedback, promoting a sense of accountability and encouraging quality service from drivers.

Tips for Efficiency

- To expedite your pick-up, choose easily accessible locations away from busy streets or construction zones, where drivers can safely reach you without unnecessary delays.
- Consider using express pooling options, which minimize detours and pick-up stops, leading to faster and more direct routes.
- Schedule rides during off-peak hours to benefit from lower demand and potentially reduced fares.

- Before requesting a ride, check for surge pricing on the app, and if applicable, wait for the surge to subside or consider alternative transportation options.
- Use the app's live status-sharing feature to inform friends or family about your ride details and estimated arrival time for safety purposes.

Cost-Saving Strategies

- Keep an eye out for promo codes, referral discounts, and special offers from the rideshare app, which can significantly reduce your overall travel expenses.
- When traveling with friends or colleagues, share the ride and split the fare, making it a cost-effective and enjoyable experience for everyone.
- Some rideshare apps offer package deals for frequent users, providing discounted rates for multiple rides within a specific timeframe.
- Integrate rideshare services with public transportation when possible, using them to cover the last leg of your journey or bridge the gap between destinations.
- Explore loyalty programs offered by rideshare companies, which may reward you with points or benefits for using their services consistently, ultimately leading to savings on future rides.

Walking and Biking in the City

Pedestrian-Friendly Areas:

Photo by Daryan Shamkhali from Unsplash

- **Central Park** – One of the city's most iconic and pedestrian-friendly spots, Central Park offers a sprawling oasis of greenery, walking paths, and scenic spots, perfect for strolls and picnics.

- **Brooklyn Bridge Promenade** – Walk along the Brooklyn Bridge promenade for breathtaking views of the Manhattan skyline and the East River, creating an unforgettable walking experience.

- **High Line Park** – A repurposed elevated railway turned into a beautiful linear park, the High Line offers a unique walking route through lush greenery and art installations, providing a tranquil escape from the bustling streets below.

- **Fifth Avenue** – Stroll along Fifth Avenue to explore high-end boutiques, cultural landmarks, and iconic architecture, showcasing the city's vibrant energy and upscale shopping scene.

- **Soho and Greenwich Village** – These charming neighborhoods are perfect for leisurely walks, boasting cobblestone streets, historic buildings, trendy shops, and a diverse mix of cafes and restaurants.

Biking in the City - Bike Rentals:

Photo by Christie Kim from Unsplash

- **Citi Bike** – New York's bike-sharing program, Citi Bike, provides a convenient and cost-effective way to explore the city on two wheels, with numerous docking stations available throughout Manhattan, Brooklyn, and Queens.

- **Bike Rental Shops** – Many bike rental shops across the city offer various types of bikes for all ages and skill levels, allowing you to customize your biking adventure.

- **Hudson River Greenway** – Take advantage of the Hudson River Greenway, a dedicated bike path along the Hudson River, offering scenic views of the water and skyline while providing a safe route for cyclists.

- **Governors Island** – Reachable by ferry, Governors Island offers car-free biking opportunities with bike rentals available on the island, providing a peaceful and scenic ride away from city traffic.

- **Brooklyn's Prospect Park** – With dedicated bike lanes and a tranquil atmosphere, Prospect Park in Brooklyn is a popular destination for cyclists seeking a relaxing and picturesque ride.

Safety Tips for Walking and Biking

Walking:

- **Crosswalks and Signals** – Always use designated crosswalks and obey traffic signals when crossing streets to ensure safety and smooth traffic flow.

- **Stay Visible at Night** – If walking at night, wear reflective clothing or accessories to enhance your visibility to drivers and cyclists.

- **Sidewalk Etiquette** – On busy sidewalks, walk on the right side to allow smooth pedestrian flow, and be mindful of others to avoid collisions.

- **Be Aware of Surroundings** – Stay alert and aware of your surroundings, keeping personal belongings secure, especially in crowded areas.

- **Use Pedestrian Paths** – Use dedicated pedestrian paths, parks, and greenways to enjoy a safer and more pleasant walking experience.

Biking:

- **Wear a Helmet** – Protect yourself by wearing a properly fitted helmet whenever cycling, regardless of your skill level or the distance you plan to ride.

- **Follow Traffic Rules** – Bicycles are considered vehicles, so obey traffic signs and signals, use appropriate hand signals for turns, and ride in the same direction as traffic.

- **Use Bike Lanes** – Stick to designated bike lanes to minimize interactions with motor vehicles and pedestrians.

- **Be Visible and Predictable** – Use lights and reflectors, especially at night, and signal your intentions clearly to alert drivers and pedestrians of your movements.

- **Avoid Rush Hour** – If you're new to biking in the city, avoid biking during rush hour when traffic is at its peak, and the streets may be more challenging to navigate.

Accommodation

Accommodation is vital in New York City (NYC) for anyone planning to stay there for more than just a day trip. NYC is a bustling metropolis with many attractions, cultural landmarks, and events, making it a popular destination for tourists and business travelers.

Choosing the Right Neighborhood

Choosing the right neighborhood is essential to ensure a satisfying and enjoyable experience in a new city. Here are some factors to consider when selecting a neighborhood:

- **Proximity to Points of Interest** – Consider your main points of interest and prioritize neighborhoods that offer easy access to those attractions. If you're into museums and art galleries, neighborhoods near museums like the Upper East Side and Chelsea may be ideal. For nightlife and entertainment, areas like the East Village or Williamsburg could be more suitable.

- **Safety and Security** – Research the safety ratings and crime statistics of the neighborhoods you're considering. Look for areas with a good reputation for safety, especially if you plan to walk around during the evenings.

- **Transportation Accessibility** – Evaluate the neighborhood's public transportation options, including subway stations, buses, and proximity to major transportation hubs. Good transportation connections can significantly improve your mobility within the city.

- **Local Amenities and Services** – Look for neighborhoods with various amenities, such as grocery stores, pharmacies, restaurants, and parks. Having essential services nearby can enhance your overall convenience and comfort during your stay.

- **Budget Considerations** – NYC offers many accommodation options, from luxury hotels to budget-friendly hostels. Set a budget for your stay and explore neighborhoods aligning with your financial plan while meeting your other preferences.

Remember that each neighborhood in NYC has its unique charm and character, so taking the time to research and find the best match for your interests and budget will ensure a more enjoyable and fulfilling stay in the city.

Hotel Options and Alternatives

New York offers various hotel options and alternatives to suit various preferences, budgets, and travel styles. Whether you're looking for luxury accommodations, budget-friendly stays, or unique and personalized experiences, NYC has something to offer for every traveler.

Here are some of the hotel options and alternatives you can find in NYC:

Boutique Hotels

- Boutique hotels are small, stylish, and often independently owned properties that offer a more personalized and intimate experience.
- These hotels usually have unique decor and furnishings, providing a distinct ambiance that sets them apart from larger chain hotels.
- Guests can expect personalized services and attention to detail, as boutique hotels aim to create a more individualized and memorable stay.
- Amenities may include on-site restaurants with locally inspired cuisine, trendy bars, and cozy lounges, contributing to a vibrant and social atmosphere.
- Boutique hotels are great for travelers seeking a more intimate, sophisticated experience with characterful surroundings.

Hostels

- Hostels are budget-friendly accommodations that offer dormitory-style rooms with shared facilities like bathrooms and communal areas.
- Ideal for solo travelers, backpackers, and budget-conscious adventurers, hostels provide a friendly environment, making it easy to meet fellow travelers.
- Some hostels also offer private rooms or smaller dorm options, catering to travelers wanting more privacy.
- Shared kitchen facilities allow guests to prepare their meals, helping save money on dining expenses.
- Hostels are an excellent option for those seeking affordability, a social atmosphere, and the opportunity to connect with like-minded travelers.

Vacation Rentals

- Vacation rentals, often available through platforms like Airbnb or VRBO, are private properties, ranging from apartments to entire houses, that can be rented for short-term stays.
- These accommodations offer a more home-like experience, providing fully furnished spaces with kitchen facilities, living areas, and bedrooms.
- Vacation rentals are suitable for families or groups of travelers who prefer the comfort and privacy of a home setting.
- Renting a vacation property can be more cost-effective for extended stays, as you can often negotiate rates or find discounts for longer bookings.
- Vacation rentals allow you to immerse yourself in residential neighborhoods, giving you a taste of local life and culture.

Bed and Breakfasts (B&Bs)

- B&Bs are typically smaller establishments run by local hosts, offering cozy rooms with breakfast included in the price.
- These accommodations provide a warm and welcoming atmosphere, and the hosts often offer valuable insights and recommendations about the local area.
- B&Bs can be found in urban and rural locations, making them an excellent choice for travelers seeking a more homey and intimate experience.
- Breakfast is usually a highlight, featuring homemade or locally sourced dishes, adding to the charm and appeal of staying at a B&B.
- B&Bs are a delightful option for travelers who appreciate a personal touch and enjoy getting to know their hosts and fellow guests.

Extended Stay Hotels

- Extended-stay hotels are designed for guests planning longer stays, offering apartment-style accommodations with kitchenettes or full kitchens.
- These hotels provide a comfortable and more spacious living environment, making them suitable for business travelers, families, or anyone requiring an extended visit.
- Guests can enjoy the convenience of in-room amenities and on-site facilities like laundry rooms, fitness centers, and business centers.
- Many extended-stay hotels offer weekly or monthly rates, which can be more cost-effective for extended trips than traditional hotels.
- Extended-stay hotels offer the comforts of home combined with the convenience and services of a hotel, making them a practical choice for travelers needing an extended stay in NYC.

Booking Tips and Resources

Booking tips and resources are essential when traveling to New York City (NYC) or any destination. NYC is a bustling and popular travel destination, and having the right booking strategies and resources can greatly enhance your travel experience.

- **Compare Multiple Platforms** – Don't limit yourself to just one website or platform when booking accommodation, flights, or activities. Compare prices and offerings across multiple platforms, such as travel booking websites, hotel aggregators, and airline websites, to ensure you get the best deal.

- **Flexible Travel Dates** – If your travel dates are flexible, consider using fare comparison tools or hotel search engines that show rates across a range of dates. Being open to different travel periods can lead to significant savings, especially during off-peak seasons.

- **Sign Up for Price Alerts** – Many travel websites and apps offer price alert features that notify you when prices drop for flights or accommodations to your desired destination. Signing up for these alerts can help you catch excellent deals.

- **Read Reviews and Ratings** – Review reviews and ratings from previous travelers before booking any accommodation or activity. Platforms like TripAdvisor, Google Reviews, or Booking.com often provide valuable insights from real guests, helping you make informed choices.

- **Consider Package Deals** – Explore deals that combine flights, accommodation, and activities for added convenience and savings. Travel agencies and online platforms often offer package options, which can be more cost-effective than booking each element separately.

Remember that prices and availability can fluctuate, so booking well in advance for popular destinations or travel seasons is best. Additionally, be cautious of overly enticing deals that seem too good to be true, and always review the cancellation policies before finalizing your bookings.

Safety and Etiquette

NYC is a bustling metropolis with a diverse population and many tourists. Being vigilant and practicing safety measures can help protect you from potential risks such as pickpocketing, scams, or petty crime in busy urban areas.

Staying Safe in the City

Staying Safe in the City: General Safety Tips

- **Stay in Well-Lit and Crowded Areas** – Stick to well-lit and populated streets, especially during the evening and night. Avoid poorly lit or deserted areas, which may pose higher safety risks.

- **Keep Valuables Secure** – Keep your valuables, such as wallets, phones, and cameras, secure and out of sight, preferably in a crossbody bag or a front pocket. Avoid displaying expensive jewelry or electronics to minimize the risk of theft.

- **Use Reliable Transportation** – Opt for licensed and reputable transportation services like official taxis or rideshare apps. Avoid accepting rides from unmarked vehicles or individuals without proper identification.

- **Share Your Itinerary** – Inform a trusted friend or family member of your travel plans, including your itinerary and accommodation details. Regularly check in with them, especially if you're exploring the city alone.

- **Stay Aware of Your Surroundings** – Always be observant and aware of your surroundings. Avoid distractions from electronic devices when walking, especially in crowded areas, to minimize the risk of accidents or theft.

Avoiding Scams

- **Be Cautious of Strangers** – Be cautious when approached by strangers offering unsolicited help or goods, as this could be a common tactic used in scams.

- **Ignore Unsolicited Offers** – Avoid engaging with street performers, street vendors, or individuals offering free items, as they might expect payment afterward or use distraction techniques to steal from you.

- **Beware of "Found" Items** – If someone "finds" money or valuable items and offers to share them with you, decline politely and walk away. It's often a setup to get money or personal information from unsuspecting tourists.

- **Verify Prices and Bills** – Double-check prices before purchasing, and ensure you receive the correct change. Some scams involve overcharging or giving counterfeit money as change.

- **ATM Safety** – Use ATMs located within banks or reputable establishments, and cover your PIN when entering it. Be cautious of anyone trying to "help" you with the ATM, as they may be attempting to steal your information.

Being Aware of Your Surroundings

- **Plan Routes in Advance** – Plan your routes before venturing out, especially if you're unfamiliar with the area. Knowing where you're going can help you navigate confidently and avoid getting lost.

- **Ask for Directions from Official Sources** – If you need directions, seek assistance from official information centers, hotel concierges, or uniformed law enforcement officers.

- **Trust Your Instincts** - If something feels uncomfortable or unsafe, trust your instincts and remove yourself. Avoid engaging with individuals who make you feel uneasy.

- **Use Crosswalks and Obey Signals** - Cross streets at designated crosswalks and wait for the pedestrian signals to change before crossing. Avoid jaywalking, as it can be dangerous and may result in fines.

- **Avoid Excessive Alcohol Consumption** - If you plan to enjoy the city's nightlife, drink responsibly and be cautious of accepting drinks from strangers. Excessive alcohol consumption can impair judgment and make you more vulnerable to potential risks.

New York City Etiquette

- **Cultural Diversity** - NYC is a melting pot of cultures and backgrounds. Embrace the city's diversity by respecting different customs, languages, and traditions you may encounter.

- **Tipping Practices** - Tipping is customary in NYC for various services, such as restaurants, bars, hotels, and taxis. It's typical to leave a gratuity of around 15-20% of the total bill for good service in restaurants. Check if a service charge is already included before tipping in other establishments.

- **Sidewalk Etiquette** - NYC sidewalks can get crowded, so be mindful of your walking pace and avoid abruptly stopping in the middle of the sidewalk. Stay to the right to allow smooth pedestrian flow, especially during rush hours.

- **Respecting Personal Space** - NYC is a densely populated city, and personal space can be limited, especially in public transportation. Be conscious of others' personal space and avoid unnecessary physical contact or crowding.

- **Volume and Noise Levels** – While NYC is lively and vibrant, be mindful of your noise levels, especially in residential areas and public spaces like libraries and museums. Use headphones when listening to music or watching videos in public to avoid disturbing others.

Seasonal Considerations and Weather Tips

Spring (March to May):

- Weather – Spring in NYC is mild, with temperatures ranging from cool to warm. Be prepared for occasional rain showers during this season.
- Seasonal Events – Enjoy the cherry blossoms in Central Park and various outdoor festivals and parades, such as the St. Patrick's Day Parade and the Tribeca Film Festival.
- Attire – Layered clothing is essential during spring, as temperatures vary throughout the day. Bring a mix of light sweaters, jackets, and a waterproof layer for unexpected showers.

Summer (June to August):

- Weather – Summers in NYC are hot and humid, with temperatures often reaching the 80s and 90s Fahrenheit. Heatwaves are common.
- Seasonal Events – Experience outdoor concerts, Shakespeare in the Park, and Fourth of July fireworks.
- Attire – Dress in lightweight, breathable clothing such as shorts, T-shirts, dresses, and sandals. Don't forget to wear sunscreen, a wide-brimmed hat, and sunglasses to protect yourself from the sun.

Fall (September to November):

- Weather – Fall brings cooler temperatures to NYC, with crisp and pleasant days. It's a beautiful time to visit as the leaves change color.
- Seasonal Events – Enjoy the New York Film Festival, Halloween festivities, and Thanksgiving parades.
- Attire – Pack layers, including sweaters, scarves, and a light jacket, as temperatures can fluctuate during the day. Comfortable walking shoes are essential for exploring the city.

Winter (December to February):

- Weather – Winters in NYC are cold, with temperatures often below freezing. Snow and icy conditions are possible.
- Seasonal Events – Experience the festive atmosphere of holiday markets, the Rockefeller Center Christmas Tree lighting, and ice skating at iconic locations.
- Attire – Bring warm winter coats, hats, gloves, and insulated boots. Layering is key, so include sweaters and thermal wear to stay comfortable in the chilly weather.

Year-Round Tips:

- Umbrella and Rain Gear – It's always a good idea to carry a compact umbrella and rainproof footwear, as rain showers can occur throughout the year.
- Comfortable Walking Shoes – NYC is a walking city, so comfortable and supportive shoes are essential to explore its neighborhoods and attractions.
- Public Indoor Spaces – During extreme weather conditions, such as heatwaves or winter storms, seek refuge in public indoor spaces like museums, shopping malls, and restaurants.

This chapter discussed essential considerations for traveling to New York City. We covered the significance of transportation options, including airports, public transportation, rideshare services, and walking or biking around the city. We explored the importance of choosing the right neighborhood based on interests, safety, and budget. Additionally, we provided valuable tips for booking accommodations, flights, and activities to ensure a smooth and enjoyable trip.

The upcoming chapter will delve into the iconic landmarks and monuments that make New York City an extraordinary destination. We'll discover these architectural marvels' historical and cultural significance, from the Statue of Liberty to the Empire State Building. We will also explore lesser-known monuments and their hidden stories, guiding you through a journey of the city's rich history and breathtaking landmarks.

Get ready to immerse yourself in the wonders that make NYC a truly remarkable place.

CHAPTER 3

Landmarks & Monuments

Photo by Redd F from Unsplash

Did you know that the Statue of Liberty, an iconic symbol of freedom and democracy, stands at an impressive height of 305 feet, making it taller than the Statue of Liberty in Paris?

New York City, the city that never sleeps, boasts a plethora of awe-inspiring landmarks and monuments that have captured the imaginations of millions around the globe.

In this chapter, we will embark on a journey through the rich history and cultural significance of these renowned landmarks, delving into the stories that have shaped the identity of this vibrant metropolis.

From the historic Ellis Island to the grandeur of Central Park, join us as we unravel the secrets and marvels of these extraordinary sites that have shaped the Big Apple into the captivating city it is today.

Landmarks in Staten Island

Staten Island, one of the five boroughs of New York City, is home to several notable landmarks and attractions. While it may not have as many famous landmarks as Manhattan, Staten Island still offers a variety of interesting sites and destinations worth exploring.

Staten Island Ferry

Photo by wallpaperflare.com

Unique Exhibits and Panoramic Views – The Staten Island Ferry offers a fascinating exhibit called "The Forgotten People," showcasing the history and stories of immigrants who passed through Ellis Island from 1892 to 1954. Learn about the diverse experiences that shaped the city's identity.

As you cruise along the harbor, enjoy breathtaking panoramic sights of the Manhattan skyline, as well as iconic landmarks such as the One World Trade Center, the Empire State Building, and the Brooklyn Bridge.

Wildlife Spotting – Watch for marine life during the ferry ride! Lucky travelers might glimpse playful dolphins or majestic seagulls soaring overhead. The waters surrounding the ferry route are teeming with marine activity, offering a chance to witness the natural beauty of the New York Harbor.

Family-Friendly Activities – On board the ferry, families can enjoy a stroll along the outdoor decks, basking in the fresh sea breeze while taking in the scenic sights. Children can participate in the Junior Ranger program, where they can engage in fun and educational activities related to the history and ecology of the New York Harbor.

Iconic Photo Opportunities - Capture picture-perfect moments with the Statue of Liberty as your backdrop. The ferry ride provides some of the best photo opportunities to cherish those unforgettable memories. Snapshots of the Verrazzano-Narrows Bridge, one of the longest suspension bridges in the world, connecting Staten Island to Brooklyn, and admire its remarkable engineering.

Nighttime Magic – For a magical experience, consider taking the Staten Island Ferry at night. The city lights create a dazzling spectacle that transforms the skyline into a mesmerizing display of colors.

Statue of Liberty

Photo by Pexels

Unique Exhibits and Historical Insights – The Statue of Liberty Museum houses an impressive collection of exhibits and artifacts, delving into the history and construction of this iconic monument. Discover the remarkable story of how France gifted this symbol of freedom to the United States.

Explore the "Inspiration Gallery," where you can learn about the immigrants' journeys and their pursuit of the American dream.

Up Close with Lady Liberty – Ascend to the statue's pedestal or, for a more thrilling experience, venture to the crown observation deck (accessible by reservation). From either vantage point, enjoy breathtaking views of the city and harbor.

Family-Friendly Activities – The Statue of Liberty National Monument offers engaging Junior Ranger programs for children, allowing them to interact with rangers and learn about the monument's significance in a fun and interactive way. Families can enjoy a relaxing picnic on Liberty Island's grounds while admiring the majestic statue.

Statue by Night – Experience the enchanting ambiance of the Statue of Liberty at night by taking an evening tour. Witness the statue illuminated against the dark sky, creating an awe-inspiring sight.

Statue Cruises – Consider taking a Statue Cruise, including stops at Liberty Island and Ellis Island. This comprehensive experience allows you to explore the Statue of Liberty and the Ellis Island National Museum of Immigration, delving into the history of millions of immigrants who passed through its halls.

Landmarks in Manhattan

Manhattan, the heart of New York City, is a treasure trove of iconic landmarks that define its skyline and charm. From soaring skyscrapers to expansive green spaces, the island offers diverse attractions to explore. Join us as we delve into the fascinating world of Manhattan's landmarks and uncover the hidden gems.

Empire State Building

Photo by Paphop W. from Pexels

- Standing at 1,454 feet tall, the Empire State Building was once the tallest in the world and remains an architectural marvel of its time.
- Its Art Deco design, featuring impressive setbacks and a distinctive spire, continues to captivate visitors with its timeless elegance.
- The Empire State Building's observation deck on the 86th floor offers 360-degree views of Manhattan, providing a breathtaking panorama of the city's skyline.

- Visitors can use high-powered binoculars to examine notable landmarks and neighborhoods closely.
- Arriving early in the morning or later in the evening can help you avoid peak visiting hours and enjoy a more relaxed experience. Consider purchasing the Express Pass to skip the regular lines and maximize your time.

Central Park

Photo by Amelia from Unsplash

- Bethesda Terrace and Fountain is a stunning architectural marvel with beautiful lake views.
- The Central Park Zoo offers diverse animals and interactive exhibits for families.
- Take a stroll or rent a bike to traverse the scenic pathways and bridges that wind through the park. Enjoy a peaceful boat ride on Central Park Lake, where you can row past picturesque landscapes.

- The North Woods, a secluded woodland area with waterfalls and rustic bridges, provides a tranquil escape from the bustling city.
- Conservatory Garden is a hidden gem with beautifully manicured gardens, fountains, and serene walking paths.

Times Square

Photo by Vidar Nordli-Mathisen from Unsplash

- The dazzling Broadway theaters, where you can catch world-class performances and musicals.
- The iconic New Year's Eve Ball Drop attracts thousands of revelers to celebrate the countdown.
- Immerse yourself in the vibrant atmosphere as the dazzling electronic billboards light up the night sky.
- Visit the Times Square Museum & Visitor Center to learn about the area's history and its evolution into a global entertainment hub.
- Duffy Square is a triangular plaza featuring the TKTS booth, where you can purchase discounted Broadway show tickets. Restaurant Row on West 46th Street is a hidden culinary delight offering various dining options.

One World Trade Center

Photo by Pexels

- The 9/11 Memorial & Museum is a poignant tribute to September 11, 2001, and the lives lost.
- The Sky Pod Elevators whisking visitors to the top in just 60 seconds, with immersive displays showcasing the evolution of New York City.
- Experience "See Forever Theater," a dynamic presentation that provides an emotional journey through the city's history.
- Step onto the Sky Portal, a unique viewing platform with a thrilling real-time perspective of the bustling streets below.
- Westfield World Trade Center is an underground shopping mall featuring many retail outlets and dining options.

Rockefeller Center

Photo by Bobby Mikul

- Top of the Rock Observation Deck offers unparalleled Manhattan views, including the Empire State Building and Central Park. The iconic Christmas Tree Lighting Ceremony is a festive tradition that draws crowds worldwide during the holiday season.
- Take a guided tour of NBC Studios, where you can get a behind-the-scenes look at your favorite television shows.
- In the winter, enjoy ice skating at the famous Rockefeller Center Ice Rink, a classic New York City experience.
- The Channel Gardens is an elegant promenade with beautiful seasonal displays and sculptures.
- The underground Concourse is a hidden walkway connecting Rockefeller Center to various subway lines and nearby buildings.

Chrysler Building

Photo by Guy Percival

- Admire the stunning Art Deco design of the Chrysler Building, characterized by its distinctive terraced crown and steel gargoyles.
- The lobby features exquisite marble artwork and intricate metalwork, transporting visitors to the glamour of the 1930s.
- Though the Chrysler Building is primarily an office building, occasional art exhibitions, and displays can be found in the lobby.
- Look for historical artifacts and memorabilia related to its construction and significance in the city's skyline.
- The Chrysler Building was briefly the tallest in the world before being surpassed by the Empire State Building in 1931. Its gleaming stainless-steel spire was secretly assembled

inside the building before being raised into place, making it a technological marvel of its time.

Broadway Theaters

Photo by MikeJiroch

- The Theater District is synonymous with Broadway, the world-famous theater district where you can catch award-winning musicals and plays.
- Experience the magic of live performances at iconic venues like the Gershwin Theatre, home to the long-running hit "Wicked," or the Majestic Theatre, where "The Phantom of the Opera" enchants audiences.
- Explore the Theater District's various museums and exhibits dedicated to the history of Broadway and its legendary stars.
- Visit the Broadway Museum to see rare costumes, props, and memorabilia from classic shows.
- Introduce your kids to the theater world through family-friendly productions and interactive workshops for young theater enthusiasts.

Grand Central Terminal

Photo by Mike Peel

- Marvel at the stunning Beaux-Arts architecture of Grand Central Terminal, featuring a grand concourse with an astronomical mural on the ceiling.
- Admire the iconic four-faced brass clock in the center of the concourse, a popular meeting spot for visitors and New Yorkers alike.
- The New York Transit Museum Gallery Annex and Store within Grand Central Terminal offers fascinating exhibits on the history of the city's transportation system. Don't miss the exhibit on constructing and preserving Grand Central Terminal itself.
- Kids will love the Whispering Gallery, an acoustic marvel near the Oyster Bar & Restaurant, where whispers along the arched walls can be heard from across the room.
- Check out special events and art installations in Vanderbilt Hall, a magnificent space known for hosting various exhibitions and activities.

Landmarks in Brooklyn

Brooklyn, a vibrant borough of New York City, is a treasure trove of diverse landmarks and attractions that showcase its unique culture and history. From iconic bridges to thrilling amusement parks, Brooklyn offers something for everyone to explore and enjoy.

Join us as we uncover the charm and excitement of Brooklyn's renowned landmarks.

Brooklyn Bridge

Photo by wallpaperflare.com

- The Brooklyn Bridge, completed in 1883, is one of the oldest suspension bridges in the United States and a symbol of engineering excellence. Designed by John A. Roebling, the bridge's distinctive Gothic arches and granite towers make it a sight to behold.
- Experience the magic of the Brooklyn Bridge by taking a stroll across its elevated pedestrian walkway.

- Capture breathtaking views of the Manhattan skyline, the East River, and the Statue of Liberty.
- Head to the Brooklyn Bridge Park near the bridge's Brooklyn-side entrance for fantastic photo opportunities and green spaces to relax.
- Brooklyn Heights Promenade offers an elevated vantage point with stunning views of the Brooklyn Bridge and Manhattan's skyline.

Coney Island

Photo by Rhododendrites

- Coney Island is renowned for its historic amusement park, Luna Park, which boasts thrilling rides like the Cyclone roller coaster and the Wonder Wheel. Enjoy a mix of classic and modern attractions, entertaining visitors of all ages.
- Coney Island's sandy beach invites you to relax and soak up the sun while taking in the vibrant atmosphere of the boardwalk.

- Take a refreshing dip in the Atlantic Ocean or participate in beachside activities like volleyball and sandcastle building.
- Don't miss the Coney Island Museum, where you can explore the history and nostalgia of this iconic seaside destination.
- Stroll along the boardwalk to find various quirky shops, arcades, and eateries that add to the unique charm of Coney Island.

Barclays Center

Photo by Tdorante10

- Barclays Center often hosts art exhibitions and special events, showcasing works from local and international artists. Keep an eye out for rotating exhibits that offer a diverse range of artistic expressions.
- As the home of the Brooklyn Nets (NBA) and the New York Islanders (NHL), Barclays Center is the place to catch thrilling basketball and hockey games.
- Experience world-class concerts and performances by renowned artists and entertainers.

- Enjoy family-friendly events like circus shows, ice skating extravaganzas, and other spectacles at the center.
- The KidZone, an interactive play area for children, offers a fun-filled space to burn off energy before or after events.

Brooklyn Botanic Garden

Photo by Andre Carrotflower

- The Brooklyn Botanic Garden hosts seasonal exhibits and events like the Cherry Blossom Festival, showcasing stunning cherry blossoms in spring.
- Don't miss the Fragrance Garden, where visitors can experience a sensory journey through aromatic plants.
- Children will love the Discovery Garden, a hands-on area that encourages interactive learning and exploration of nature.
- Look for family programs and workshops to engage young minds in horticulture and environmental stewardship.

- Escape the city's hustle and bustle by strolling through the serene Japanese Hill-and-Pond Garden, featuring a picturesque landscape and a red torii gate.

Prospect Park

Photo by Badtartin

- Prospect Park hosts various art installations and exhibits that add an artistic touch to this natural oasis.
- Keep an eye on their event calendar for temporary installations and interactive displays.
- Prospect Park Zoo is a must-visit, where children can encounter a variety of animals and learn about wildlife conservation.
- The LeFrak Center at Lakeside offers seasonal ice skating in winter and roller skating in warmer months, providing endless family fun.
- Explore the Long Meadow, a vast open space perfect for picnics, sports, and kite-flying during warmer months. The Audubon Center and Boathouse offer educational programs and nature-themed activities for all ages.

New York Aquarium

Photo by Allie Caulfield

- The New York Aquarium showcases diverse marine life, including sharks, sea lions, penguins, and more.
- The Ocean Wonders: Sharks! exhibit offers a thrilling immersive experience with a tunnel surrounded by sharks and other aquatic creatures.
- Don't miss the daily sea lion and penguin feedings, where you can observe these playful creatures up close and learn about their behaviors.
- The Aquatheater performances provide educational and entertaining shows featuring dolphins and other marine animals.
- The aquarium offers various interactive exhibits and touch pools, allowing children to engage with marine life in a safe and educational environment. Join guided tours and workshops to deepen your understanding of marine conservation and ocean ecosystems.

Landmarks in Queens

Queens, the largest borough of New York City, is a melting pot of cultures and a haven for landmarks and attractions that showcase its diversity and natural beauty. From expansive parks to unique sports venues, Queens offers a multitude of exciting destinations for visitors of all ages. Let's explore some of the must-visit landmarks in Queens.

Flushing Meadows - Corona Park

Photo by Emma Angel on Unsplash

- The Queens Museum, located within Flushing Meadows - Corona Park, houses the famous Panorama of the City of New York. This impressive scale model of the city offers a bird's-eye view of all five boroughs.
- Marvel at the iconic Unisphere, a massive steel globe that served as the centerpiece of the 1964-1965 New York World's Fair.

- The Queens Zoo in the park features animals from the Americas, including bison, mountain lions, and playful sea lions.
- Take a leisurely walk through the Aviary, where you can interact with a diverse collection of birds in a naturalistic setting.
- Explore the Queens Botanical Garden, an oasis of flora and fauna with themed gardens, educational programs, and seasonal events for children and families. Enjoy a relaxing paddleboat ride on the park's Meadow Lake, providing the whole family with a delightful and serene experience.

Jamaica Bay Wildlife Refuge

Photo by 灰飛作蝶

- The Jamaica Bay Wildlife Refuge Visitor Center provides interactive exhibits and educational displays about the diverse ecosystem of Jamaica Bay.
- Learn about the migratory birds that visit the refuge during different seasons and their crucial role in the ecosystem.

- The refuge is a birdwatcher's paradise, with over 330 bird species observed yearly. During your visit, spot egrets, herons, and even the elusive bald eagle.
- Watch for horseshoe crabs along the shoreline during their annual spawning season, a fascinating natural phenomenon.
- Embark on guided nature walks and ranger-led programs that cater to families, providing informative and engaging experiences for children and adults alike.

Citi Field

Photo by redlegsfan21

- Citi Field, the home of the New York Mets baseball team, showcases memorabilia and exhibits celebrating the team's history and notable players. Check out the Mets Hall of Fame & Museum for a comprehensive journey through the team's iconic moments.
- Catch an exciting baseball game with the family, and enjoy the energetic atmosphere and cheering crowds.

- The stadium hosts family-friendly events, including kids' days, where young fans can engage in fun activities and meet team mascots.
- Citi Field boasts a diverse selection of food vendors and concessions, offering an array of delicious stadium snacks and meals.
- Enjoy live music and entertainment on game days, adding to the lively ambiance of the stadium experience.

Landmarks in The Bronx

The Bronx, often called the "Borough of Parks," is home to many landmarks celebrating its rich cultural heritage and natural beauty. From world-class zoos to legendary sports stadiums, The Bronx offers diverse attractions for visitors of all ages. Let's journey through some of The Bronx's most captivating landmarks.

The Bronx Zoo

Photo by Postdlf

- The Bronx Zoo is one of the largest metropolitan zoos in the world, featuring over 6,000 animals representing various species from around the globe.
- Don't miss the Congo Gorilla Forest, an immersive exhibit where you can observe gorillas, mandrills, and other African animals in a lush rainforest setting.

- Participate in the zoo's popular Wild Encounters program, offering unique opportunities to meet animals up close and learn from zookeepers and experts.
- The Children's Zoo allows young visitors to interact with friendly farm animals, making it a delightful experience for the whole family.
- The Bronx Zoo offers various family-friendly activities, including nature-themed scavenger hunts and educational programs for children of all ages. Hop aboard the Wild Asia Monorail for a guided tour through the zoo's Asian exhibits, providing a close-up look at elephants, tigers, and more.

Yankee Stadium

Photo by Sergeant Matt Hecht

- Yankee Stadium, the legendary home of the New York Yankees, pays homage to the team's illustrious history with various exhibits and memorabilia.
- Visit the Yankees Museum, showcasing the team's championship trophies, historical artifacts, and iconic moments in baseball history.

- Catch a thrilling baseball game with the family, and experience the electrifying atmosphere of cheering fans.
- The stadium often hosts special family nights and promotions, offering young fans the chance to meet players and mascots.
- Yankee Stadium offers various food options, including traditional ballpark fare and local culinary favorites.

Edgar Allan Poe Cottage

Photo by JHSmithArch

- The Edgar Allan Poe Cottage is a historic landmark and museum, once the final home of the renowned American author and poet.
- The museum houses artifacts, manuscripts, and personal belongings of Edgar Allan Poe, providing insight into his life and literary works.
- Take a guided tour of the cottage to learn about Poe's time in The Bronx and the inspiration behind some of his most famous writings.

- The cottage hosts family-friendly events, including storytelling sessions and workshops, introducing young visitors to Poe's eerie and captivating tales.
- The Edgar Allan Poe Cottage occasionally hosts literary events, poetry readings, and performances that celebrate the works of Poe and other authors.

This chapter has taken us on a remarkable journey through the diverse landmarks of New York City's boroughs, showcasing their historical significance, cultural heritage, and natural splendor. From iconic structures like the Empire State Building and the Statue of Liberty to the enchanting beauty of Central Park and the Bronx Zoo, each landmark has left an indelible mark on the city's identity.

The next chapter will lead us to an exciting exploration of New York City's neighborhoods and districts as we move forward. From the artistic hub of Greenwich Village to the trendy streets of Williamsburg, we will delve into the unique characteristics and hidden gems that make each neighborhood a vibrant and integral part of the Big Apple's tapestry.

Let's dive into the diverse and captivating neighborhoods of New York City, where history, culture, and creativity converge in a melting pot of experiences.

CHAPTER 4

Neighborhoods and Boroughs

Photo by Pexels

Amidst the sprawling metropolis of New York City, where skyscrapers kissed the heavens, and the buzz of yellow taxis echoed through the bustling streets, a neighborhood seemed to possess a heartbeat all its own. It was where culture and diversity thrived, the scent of freshly brewed coffee mingled with the aroma of exotic spices from far-off lands, and children's laughter echoed against the backdrop of lively street art. That was the vibrant heart of the city, a place that embodied the essence of what it meant to be a New Yorker.

Nestled within the boroughs, this enchanting neighborhood was a mosaic of life, where the old and the new danced perfectly. Its streets were a labyrinth of colors and cultures, revealing the rich tapestry of its inhabitants' stories. Here, you could find the quintessential

New York brownstones, their stoops serving as a communal stage for neighbors to gather and share tales of their day. Next to them stood modern glass towers, where young professionals forged paths of success in the city that never slept.

In the mornings, the aroma of freshly baked bagels wafted through the air, drawing locals and visitors alike to the neighborhood's charming cafes. As the sun dipped below the horizon, the streets came alive with the symphony of music from street performers and the rhythm of tap-dancing shoes on worn-out pavements. It was where time seemed to slow down, inviting everyone to savor each moment and embrace the unyielding spirit of unity that bound them together.

But, like any thriving community, this vibrant neighborhood had its challenges. The rapid pulse of change coursed through its veins, testing the resilience of the locals who had called this place home for generations. Gentrification and modernization wrestled with tradition and history, painting an intricate portrait of the struggle for identity.

As the years passed, this microcosm of New York City evolved, yet the heartbeat of the neighborhood remained strong. With its steadfast sense of belonging, the people here forged unbreakable bonds, forming a tight-knit community where everyone knew your name and story. From the local bodega owner who had seen it all to the mural artist who painted dreams onto every blank wall, each person added their brushstroke to the masterpiece that was this remarkable neighborhood.

In this chapter, we embark on a journey through the neighborhoods and boroughs of New York City, starting with this enchanting and dynamic heart. As we traverse the city's tapestry of cultures and histories, we will discover the hidden gems, the iconic landmarks, and the fascinating stories that weave together to create the one-of-a-kind New York mosaic.

So, let's venture forth and delve into the diverse neighborhoods and boroughs that shape the very soul of this awe-inspiring city.

Manhattan

Times Square

Photo by Unsplash

Times Square is renowned for its dazzling and larger-than-life billboards that light up the night sky. These LED screens and digital displays showcase advertisements, movie trailers, and promotional content for various brands and events.

- The famous electronic billboards, such as the Coca-Cola sign and the NASDAQ Tower, are major landmarks that have become symbols of Times Square's vibrant energy.
- As the heart of the Theater District, Times Square is home to numerous Broadway theaters, attracting theater enthusiasts worldwide. This area boasts famous theaters, including the historic Lyceum Theatre and the majestic New Amsterdam Theatre.
- The district offers a wide range of musicals, plays, and performances, making it a hub for the performing arts.

- Just steps away from Times Square, visitors can explore the dazzling lights of Broadway, taking in the magic of live performances.
- The bustling neighborhood also offers a chance to visit popular attractions like Madame Tussauds, Ripley's Believe It or Not! Museum and the National Geographic Encounter: Ocean Odyssey, providing unique and interactive experiences.

Greenwich Village

Photo by Felix Stahlberg

Greenwich Village has a rich history of being a haven for artists, writers, and musicians, contributing to its bohemian atmosphere. This neighborhood exudes a unique charm and creative spirit that has attracted countless artists over the years.

It played a pivotal role in the Beat Generation and became a focal point for counterculture movements in the 1950s and 1960s.

- The Washington Square Arch is a prominent landmark in Greenwich Village, symbolizing its history and its role as a center for free expression and activism.

- The Village is dotted with historic brownstones and buildings that date back to the 19th century, preserving its rich architectural heritage.
- Greenwich Village offers an array of culinary delights, from quaint cafes and bistros to innovative restaurants with diverse cuisines. It's famous for its pizza, with several iconic pizzerias serving up New York-style slices that have become legendary.
- This iconic park serves as the heart of the neighborhood, providing a green oasis for locals and visitors alike. It's a hub of activity featuring street performers, chess players, and people enjoying the serene surroundings.
- Greenwich Village's history as a bohemian enclave extends to its vibrant music and nightlife scene. The Village was a hotbed for folk music in the 1960s, and famous venues like The Bitter End and Cafe Wha? still host live performances, attracting music enthusiasts from all over.

Harlem

Photo by wallpaperflare.com

Harlem is a cultural powerhouse known for its significant contributions to African American art, literature, and music. It was pivotal in the Harlem Renaissance, a period of great cultural and intellectual growth for African Americans in the early 20th century.

- Harlem's music legacy is legendary, with its jazz clubs and venues showcasing some of the most talented musicians in history, including Duke Ellington, Billie Holiday, and Louis Armstrong.
- The Apollo Theater, a historic landmark, has been the stage for countless legendary performances and continues to host music, comedy, and dance events.
- Harlem is a haven for soul food enthusiasts, offering a delectable array of Southern cuisine. Restaurants and eateries serve classics like fried chicken, collard greens, macaroni and cheese, and sweet potato pie, providing a true taste of comfort and tradition.
- Harlem is home to numerous historic sites, including the Abyssinian Baptist Church and the Studio Museum, which celebrate the neighborhood's rich cultural heritage. Visitors can explore the Hamilton Grange National Memorial, the former home of Alexander Hamilton, a founding father of the United States.
- Harlem's strong sense of community is evident in its vibrant street festivals and parades, such as the African American Day Parade and the Harlem Week celebrations. These events unite locals and visitors, fostering unity and celebrating the neighborhood's heritage and achievements.

Brooklyn

Brooklyn, the vibrant borough across the East River from Manhattan, has evolved from being New York City's best-kept secret to a cultural hotspot in its own right. Boasting diverse neighborhoods, artistic expression, and rich history, Brooklyn offers a unique and exciting experience for locals and visitors alike.

Williamsburg

Photo by streetlab.org

Williamsburg is synonymous with hipster culture, attracting creative and trendsetting individuals worldwide. The neighborhood's artistic spirit is reflected in its unique fashion, indie music scene, and innovative start-ups.

- Williamsburg's streets serve as an ever-changing canvas for street artists. Colorful murals, graffiti, and thought-provoking installations adorn walls throughout the neighborhood.

- Foodies flock to Williamsburg to savor its diverse culinary scene. The neighborhood is a haven for trendy eateries, farm-to-table restaurants, and experimental dining experiences.
- When the sun sets, Williamsburg's vibrant nightlife comes alive. The neighborhood boasts an eclectic mix of bars, music venues, and rooftop lounges.
- It's a hotspot for live performances, ranging from indie bands to up-and-coming artists, making it a go-to destination for music enthusiasts.
- Williamsburg's prime location along the East River provides stunning views of the Manhattan skyline. The waterfront parks and promenades offer a serene escape from the bustling city.

DUMBO (Down Under the Manhattan Bridge Overpass)

Photo by pxfuel.com

DUMBO's waterfront, with its iconic cobblestone streets, offers a picture-perfect view of the Manhattan Bridge and the Manhattan skyline across the river. The area's transformation from industrial to chic has become a favorite spot for locals and tourists to enjoy a stroll or a relaxing afternoon by the water.

- DUMBO is a hub for contemporary art, hosting numerous art galleries and studios. It's a vibrant community for artists and art lovers, fostering creativity and expression.
- From the Brooklyn Bridge Park, visitors can capture breathtaking views of the Brooklyn Bridge and the Manhattan skyline. It's a popular spot for photography and a serene place to unwind.
- DUMBO's charm lies in its preserved historic architecture, with converted warehouses and industrial buildings housing stylish lofts, offices, and boutiques.
- The neighborhood seamlessly blends its industrial past with contemporary design, creating a captivating urban landscape.
- One of DUMBO's delightful attractions is Jane's Carousel, a beautifully restored 1920s carousel that offers a nostalgic ride for children and adults.

Park Slope

Photo by Mikeruggy

Park Slope is renowned for its tree-lined streets adorned with elegant brownstone houses. The neighborhood's architecture reflects its historical significance and 19th-century charm. The picturesque blocks offer a glimpse into the past, making it a favorite location for strolls.

- Park Slope is adjacent to the stunning Prospect Park, designed by Frederick Law Olmsted and Calvert Vaux, who also created Central Park.
- The park offers a serene escape from the city's hustle and bustle, with walking trails, picnic spots, a zoo, and a boathouse.

- Park Slope is a popular choice for families due to its abundance of family-friendly attractions. It has various playgrounds, children's museums, and kid-centric cafes.
- The neighborhood's sense of community and safety make it an inviting place for families to call home.
- Park Slope embraces a diverse community, offering a wide range of international cuisines, boutique shops, and cultural events celebrating its multicultural residents. The neighborhood's inclusivity and openness contribute to its warm and welcoming ambiance.

Queens

Queens, the largest borough in New York City, is a melting pot of cultures and a treasure trove of diverse experiences. From its eclectic neighborhoods to its flourishing arts scene, Queens offers a captivating blend of tradition, modernity, and community spirit.

Astoria

Photo by NickCPrior

Astoria is a paradise for food enthusiasts, with many restaurants serving cuisines worldwide. The neighborhood caters to every palate, from authentic Greek tavernas to Middle Eastern eateries and trendy cafes.

- Foodies can embark on a culinary journey, exploring the streets of family-owned establishments offering traditional dishes from different cultures.
- Astoria is home to various cultural institutions celebrating art, history, and performance. The Museum of the Moving Image showcases the evolution of film and television, while

the Socrates Sculpture Park presents outdoor art exhibitions against a backdrop of Manhattan's skyline.

- The neighborhood's thriving arts community is also evident in its numerous galleries and creative spaces.
- Astoria's waterfront along the East River provides breathtaking Manhattan skyline views. The scenic Astoria Park is a popular spot to relax, jog, or picnic while admiring the iconic cityscape across the river.
- Astoria Park is home to one of the largest public pools in the city. The Astoria Park Pool, dating back to the 1930s, offers a refreshing escape during the hot summer months, attracting locals and visitors seeking a place to cool off and enjoy recreational activities.

Long Island City

Photo by King of Hearts

Long Island City has emerged as a major cultural hub, with numerous art galleries, studios, and exhibition spaces. The neighborhood's art scene has attracted artists and creatives from various disciplines, shaping its dynamic and innovative character. The annual LIC Arts Open festival celebrates the community's creativity, inviting visitors to explore the diverse art offerings in the area.

- Long Island City's waterfront parks, such as Gantry Plaza State Park and Hunter's Point South Park, offer stunning views of the East River and Manhattan's skyline. These green spaces provide opportunities for leisure, picnics, and recreational activities, drawing residents and tourists alike to enjoy the outdoors.
- Long Island City has several hidden gems, including offbeat museums, quirky shops, and unique eateries. Visitors can stumble upon unexpected treasures while exploring the neighborhood's streets. Its industrial past has transformed into an artistic and trendy present, creating a fascinating juxtaposition of old and new.
- This popular weekend market showcases vendors selling vintage items, artisanal crafts, and delectable international cuisine.
- The LIC Flea & Food Market embodies the neighborhood's eclectic spirit and serves as a community gathering point.
- Long Island City hosts various cultural events and festivals, reflecting the diversity and creative energy of the neighborhood.

Jackson Heights

Photo by streetlab.org

Jackson Heights is celebrated for its diverse population, with residents from various countries and cultural backgrounds. The neighborhood's multicultural atmosphere is evident in its vibrant ethnic enclaves, international grocery stores, and cultural festivals.

- Jackson Heights' bustling street markets offer a sensory delight, featuring worldwide fresh produce, spices, clothing, and handicrafts. The neighborhood's open-air markets create a lively and bustling ambiance, making it a favorite spot for locals to shop and socialize.
- Food enthusiasts can embark on a global culinary adventure in Jackson Heights, sampling authentic dishes from India, Colombia, Nepal, and Tibet. The neighborhood's wide range of eateries and food stalls make it a paradise for those seeking a taste of authentic ethnic cuisine.
- Heights is known for its distinctive architectural style, featuring a mix of Tudor, Art Deco, and pre-war apartment buildings.

The neighborhood's historical architecture adds character and charm to its streets, providing a unique backdrop for residents and visitors alike.

- Jackson Heights celebrates diversity through community events and festivals, such as the annual Queens Pride Parade and Festival.
- The neighborhood's inclusive spirit fosters a sense of unity and appreciation for the diverse cultures that coexist within its borders.

In this chapter, we explored the multifaceted borough of Queens, discovering its vibrant neighborhoods, rich cultural scenes, and diverse culinary delights. From the bohemian vibe of Astoria to the thriving art community of Long Island City and the multicultural atmosphere of Jackson Heights, Queens embodies the spirit of New York City's cultural tapestry.

Now, let us venture into the next chapter, where we delve into the world of museums and art in the city that has inspired countless masterpieces and housed some of the most remarkable collections in the world.

Join us as we uncover the treasures of creativity and imagination that await within the museums and galleries of New York City.

CHAPTER 5

Museum & Art

Photo by shavnya.com from Unsplash

Have you ever stepped into a museum or an art gallery and felt an inexplicable sense of wonder washing over you?

I remember the first time I walked into a grand museum, surrounded by the whispers of history and the echoes of creativity. It was a cold, rainy afternoon, and I sought refuge from the gloomy weather within those hallowed halls. Little did I know that this visit would ignite a lifelong fascination with art and the stories it holds.

As I meandered through the exhibits, each stroke of a brush and every chiseled masterpiece seemed to come alive, reaching out across centuries to touch my soul. A peculiar painting caught my eye—an enigmatic smile gracing a woman's lips whose gaze followed me as I moved from one angle to another. Her eyes held secrets and mysteries, leaving me with an insatiable curiosity to learn more about the artist's inspiration and the true identity of the enigmatic muse.

That captivating encounter left an indelible mark on my heart, and ever since that day, I have been drawn to explore the wondrous world of museums and art. These havens of creativity are more than just repositories of artifacts and canvases; they are portals to different epochs, diverse cultures, and the deepest recesses of the human imagination.

This chapter will unravel the magic held within these cultural sanctuaries. From ancient artifacts that whisper stories of long-forgotten civilizations to contemporary masterpieces that challenge societal norms, we will delve into the essence of museums and art, seeking inspiration, knowledge, and a renewed appreciation for the beauty surrounding us.

So, grab your imaginary museum ticket, and let's wander together through the galleries of time, where each brushstroke, sculpted form, and intricate artifact beckons us to behold the world through the eyes of artists, past and present. Welcome to a realm where creativity knows no bounds and history finds its voice through the colors of the past.

Let's begin this adventure that will leave us forever enchanted by the power of Museums and Art.

Art Museums

Art museums are cultural sanctuaries that house an incredible array of artistic expressions from various eras and regions. These institutions preserve our cultural heritage and offer visitors a chance to immerse themselves in the world of creativity and imagination.

In this section, we will explore three iconic art museums that have captured the hearts of art enthusiasts worldwide.

The Metropolitan Museum of Art (The Met)

Photo by Robert Bye from Unsplash

The Met boasts an extensive collection of over two million artworks spanning 5,000 years of human history, making it one of the world's largest and most diverse art museums. Visitors can explore artworks from different civilizations, including ancient Egyptian artifacts, European Renaissance paintings, Asian sculptures, and American decorative arts.

- Among its treasures is Leonardo da Vinci's "Portrait of a Young Man," a captivating and enigmatic portrayal of youth.

- Vincent van Gogh's "Wheat Field with Cypresses" exhibits the artist's characteristic swirling brushstrokes and vibrant colors, reflecting his emotional intensity.
- The Egyptian Temple of Dendur, a massive sandstone temple gifted to the United States, offers a glimpse into ancient Egyptian architecture and beliefs.
- The Met regularly hosts special exhibitions, drawing from its extensive collection and collaborating with renowned institutions worldwide.
- Visitors can enjoy immersive experiences like thematic showcases of a particular artist, period, or artistic movement, offering fresh perspectives on art history.

Museum of Modern Art (MoMA)

Photo by Jamison McAndie from Unsplash

MoMA is a pioneer in showcasing modern and contemporary art, featuring works by influential artists like Pablo Picasso, Salvador Dali, and Jackson Pollock.

- Visitors can witness the evolution of art, from Cubism and Surrealism to Abstract Expressionism and Pop Art.

- MoMA continually pushes the boundaries of traditional exhibitions, presenting thought-provoking installations that challenge the viewers' perspectives.
- Interactive exhibits and multimedia displays enhance visitors' engagement, creating a dynamic and enriching experience.
- The museum often hosts interactive installations that invite visitors to participate and become part of the artwork, blurring the lines between observer and creator.
- Besides visual arts, MoMA also has an impressive film collection, celebrating the history and impact of cinema through screenings and film-related exhibitions.

Guggenheim Museum

Photo by Nicholas Ceglia from Unsplash

- The Guggenheim Museum, designed by architect Frank Lloyd Wright, is an architectural masterpiece. Its spiral design allows for a continuous and fluid art-viewing experience.

- The innovative structure adds a distinctive dimension to the art displayed within its walls.
- The Guggenheim's collection encompasses a wide range of artworks, focusing on Impressionist, Post-Impressionist, and Modern art, with notable pieces by artists like Wassily Kandinsky and Marc Chagall.
- As a "living museum," the Guggenheim regularly rotates its exhibitions, ensuring visitors encounter fresh and exciting artworks.
- The Guggenheim's global presence extends to its branch in Bilbao, Spain. The Guggenheim Bilbao is an architectural marvel in its own right and houses an impressive collection of contemporary art.

These art museums are not just places to observe art passively; they are gateways to cultural exploration, inspiration, and a deeper understanding of the human experience. Whether you're an art enthusiast or a casual visitor, these institutions have something extraordinary to offer, promising an enriching and unforgettable journey through the realms of creativity and imagination.

Specialized Museums

Specialized museums offer a unique and focused exploration of specific subjects, providing visitors with in-depth knowledge and captivating experiences. This section will uncover three exceptional specialized museums in New York City.

American Museum of Natural History

Photo by Aditya Vyas from Unsplash

The American Museum of Natural History enthralls visitors with lifelike dioramas, showcasing various ecosystems and their diverse creatures.

- From the African savannah to the ocean's depths, these exhibits transport visitors to far-flung corners of the Earth.
- One of the museum's most iconic attractions is its extensive collection of dinosaur fossils, including the towering Tyrannosaurus rex and the long-necked Apatosaurus.

- The dinosaur exhibits are educational and awe-inspiring, igniting the imaginations of both young and old.
- The Hayden Planetarium within the museum offers an immersive journey through space and time.
- Cutting-edge technology brings the cosmos to life, allowing visitors to witness the wonders of the universe and our place within it.

Museum of the City of New York

Photo by Beyond My Ken

The Museum of the City of New York is dedicated to preserving and showcasing the city's rich history, from its early days as a Dutch settlement to its modern cosmopolitan identity.

- Through artifacts, photographs, and multimedia presentations, visitors can trace the evolution of New York City across centuries.
- The museum houses an extensive collection of photographs, providing a visual narrative of New York City's past and present.

- Visitors can witness iconic historical moments, the diversity of its neighborhoods, and the vibrant cultural tapestry that makes the city unique.
- The exhibits celebrate the diverse cultural heritage of New York City, highlighting the contributions of various communities and the traditions that shape the city's identity.
- The museum offers interactive programs and educational workshops for visitors of all ages, encouraging active engagement with the city's history and culture.

Intrepid Sea, Air & Space Museum

Photo by Dana Andreea Gheorghe from Unsplash

- The Intrepid Museum showcases an impressive collection of aircraft, including the legendary Concorde, the supersonic passenger airliner that revolutionized air travel.
- A museum highlight is the Space Shuttle Pavilion, home to the space shuttle Enterprise—a test vehicle that paved the way for subsequent shuttle missions.

- The museum offers interactive exhibits allowing visitors to experience life on an aircraft carrier, from the flight deck to the crew's quarters.
- Visitors can step aboard the USS Growler, a Cold War-era submarine, and learn about the challenges submariners face during their missions beneath the sea.
- Aspiring aviators can test their piloting skills in the museum's flight simulators, experiencing the thrill of flying various aircraft.

These specialized museums are more than just repositories of knowledge; they offer hands-on experiences and immersive journeys, enlightening us about the wonders of our world, our past, and the limitless possibilities that await us in the cosmos and beyond.

Art Galleries and Street Art

In this section, we will explore the dynamic and ever-evolving world of art galleries and street art, where creativity finds expression both within the confines of formal spaces and on the vibrant walls of the city streets.

Chelsea Gallery District

Photo by Mick Haupt from Unsplash

Chelsea Gallery District, located in Manhattan, is a mecca for contemporary art lovers, housing an impressive concentration of art galleries showcasing works by established and emerging artists. The district's reputation as an art hub draws art enthusiasts, collectors, and critics from around the globe.

- The galleries in Chelsea display diverse artistic styles, from abstract expressionism to cutting-edge digital art, providing visitors with a comprehensive view of the contemporary art landscape.

- Each gallery boasts unique curation, offering visitors a curated journey through the ever-changing art world.
- Chelsea comes alive during art openings and gallery receptions, where visitors can mingle with artists and curators, gaining insights into the creative process behind the exhibited works.
- The district also hosts art fairs and special events that celebrate art in all its forms.
- In addition to gallery spaces, Chelsea features public art installations that transform the streets into open-air galleries, further enhancing the neighborhood's artistic ambiance.

Bushwick Collective

Photo by Diane Picchiottino from Unsplash

Bushwick Collective, situated in Brooklyn, is renowned for its captivating street art murals that adorn building facades, transforming the neighborhood into an ever-evolving outdoor gallery.

- Local and international street artists contribute their talents, creating a kaleidoscope of colorful and thought-provoking artworks.
- Beyond the murals, Bushwick houses numerous artist studios, providing a glimpse into the creative process of street artists and other contemporary creators.
- Visitors may have the opportunity to meet artists and learn about the inspirations behind their urban masterpieces.
- Bushwick's artistic spirit extends beyond the visual arts, with a thriving community of musicians, writers, and performers contributing to its vibrant and diverse cultural landscape.
- The area offers guided street art tours, where knowledgeable guides lead visitors through the neighborhood, sharing insights into the stories and meanings behind street art.

5Pointz - The Institute of Higher Burnin'

Photo by Kevin Bluer from Unsplash

- 5Pointz, once located in Long Island City, Queens, was an iconic graffiti haven where artists from around the world converged to create large-scale murals on the building's walls.

- 5Pointz was crucial in elevating graffiti as an art form, fostering creativity and expression in a supportive community.
- The site became a symbol of urban artistry and an inspiration for future street artists.
- Sadly, 5Pointz was demolished in 2014 to make way for new developments, but its legacy lives on as an emblem of the power of street art to transform urban spaces.
- Though the original building is gone, the spirit of 5Pointz endures through the 5Pointz Aerosol Art Center, an indoor space where aerosol artists can continue to create and showcase their works.

In this chapter, we've journeyed through the captivating realms of museums, art galleries, and street art, discovering the boundless expressions of human creativity. From the hallowed halls of the Metropolitan Museum of Art to the colorful streets of Bushwick, we've experienced the power of art to transcend boundaries and ignite our imagination.

But our exploration doesn't end here. The next chapter will whisk us away on a culinary adventure where flavors and aromas will delight our senses. So, put on your gastronomic hats, and let's embark on a delicious journey through culinary experiences.

CHAPTER 6

Culinary Experiences

Photo by Colin Avery from Unsplash

Hungry for an adventure that will tantalize your taste buds and take you on a gastronomic journey like no other? Get ready to indulge in a chapter that promises to satisfy your curiosity and appetite! We're diving headfirst into the culinary wonderland of New York City, where every street corner boasts a delectable surprise and every restaurant tells a unique culinary story.

Have you ever wondered how a city with diverse cultures can offer an equally diverse food scene? From the sizzling hotdog stands to the Michelin-starred restaurants, New York's culinary landscape is an intoxicating blend of flavors from every corner of the globe.

As the melting pot of cultures, this city welcomes people from all walks of life and embraces their culinary traditions, creating an array of tastes that will leave you in awe.

So, let me ask you: Are you ready to join me on a delicious expedition to explore hidden gems, feast on iconic dishes, and uncover the secrets behind the city's most mouthwatering recipes? Get your appetite and sense of adventure ready because this chapter will serve up a feast for the senses.

Let's dive into the rich tapestry of New York's culinary experiences, where every bite tells a story, and every dish celebrates culture, history, and innovation. Bon appétit!

Iconic Food Establishments

New York City is a culinary playground, and certain food establishments have become iconic symbols of the city's vibrant food culture. In this section, we'll explore some of the most beloved and renowned culinary delights that have won the hearts and appetites of locals and visitors alike.

New York-style Pizza

- **Where to Find the Best Pizza Slices** – For the quintessential New York-style pizza experience, head to "Joe's Pizza" in Greenwich Village, a no-frills joint serving thin, foldable slices that ooze with flavor. "Di Fara Pizza" in Brooklyn is a legendary spot known for its meticulously crafted pizzas topped with fresh ingredients and a sprinkling of love from the owner, Dom DeMarco.

- **Classic Toppings and Local Favorites** – A classic New York slice usually features a simple yet mouthwatering combination of tomato sauce, mozzarella cheese, and a sprinkle of oregano. Don't miss out on the "White Pizza" at "Artichoke Basille's Pizza," a rich and creamy delight topped with a mixture of cheeses, spinach, and artichokes.

- **Diverse Pizza Varieties** – New York's pizza scene embraces innovation, and you can find creative options like the Detroit-style pizza at "Emmy Squared," featuring a thick, crispy crust and gooey cheese.

- **Pizza by the Slice** – Many pizzerias offer pizza by the slice, making it easy to try different varieties without committing to a whole pie. "Mama's Too!" on the Upper West Side is known for its inventive slices and mouthwatering toppings.

- **The Pizza Rat Connection** – As you savor your pizza, you might glimpse the city's famous "Pizza Rat," an internet sensation that captured hearts worldwide, showcasing the city's love for this iconic dish.

Bagels and Delis

- **Iconic Delis** – For the quintessential New York deli experience, "Katz's Delicatessen" on the Lower East Side is a must-visit, serving towering pastrami and corned beef sandwiches that are a carnivore's delight. "Carnegie Deli" was another beloved institution. Though now closed, its legacy is a symbol of classic deli culture.

- **Bagel Varieties** - "Ess-a-Bagel" is a legendary establishment known for its chewy, hand-rolled bagels with an assortment of delicious spreads and toppings. For a taste of innovation, try the rainbow bagels at "The Bagel Store" in Williamsburg, which has garnered a massive following on social media.

- **Popular Sandwich Options** – Don't miss the iconic "Reuben" sandwich, featuring pastrami or corned beef, sauerkraut, Swiss cheese, and Russian dressing, served on rye bread. Another local favorite is the "Lox Bagel," a delicious combination of smoked salmon, cream cheese, capers, and onions on a fresh bagel.

- **Matzo Ball Soup** – While visiting Delis, don't forget to try the comforting "Matzo Ball Soup," a traditional Jewish soup with light and fluffy matzo dumplings in a flavorful broth.

- **The Classic Deli Experience** – From the boisterous atmosphere to the towering sandwich stacks, New York's delis offer an experience that transports you back in time and keeps the city's culinary traditions alive.

Street Food and Food Trucks

- **Must-Try Street Food Vendors** - "Halal Guys" started as a humble food cart and is now an international sensation, serving mouthwatering chicken and gyro platters with their famous white sauce. "Momo Delight" food truck specializes in Nepalese dumplings called momos, offering a burst of flavors and spices.

- **Diverse Cuisines** - "Calexico" food truck combines Mexican and American flavors, offering delectable tacos, burritos, and their signature "Bacon Wrapped Hot Dogs." Also, the "Korilla BBQ" brings Korean-inspired dishes to the streets, with options like spicy pork burritos and Korean barbecue tacos.

- **Hidden Gems** – Food carts and trucks can be found throughout the city in unexpected corners. Watch for local gems that might surprise you with their culinary delights.

- **Food Truck Festivals** – Street food enthusiasts can enjoy food truck festivals in various neighborhoods, where various vendors come together to offer an array of flavors.

- **Grab-and-Go Convenience** – Street food and food trucks are perfect for those on the move, providing a quick and delicious bite to fuel your urban explorations.

Ethnic Cuisine

New York City's cultural diversity is beautifully reflected in its culinary landscape, with various neighborhoods offering an array of authentic ethnic cuisines. In this section, we'll explore three iconic ethnic enclaves where you can embark on a delightful gastronomic journey.

Chinatown

Photo by Glenn Abelson from Unsplash

- **Authentic Chinese Eateries** – In the bustling streets of Chinatown, you'll find a treasure trove of authentic Chinese restaurants, ranging from family-owned establishments to vibrant eateries that showcase the rich tapestry of Chinese flavors. Don't be afraid to explore small, unassuming spots, as they often hold culinary gems that locals swear by.

- **Dim Sum Delights** – Chinatown is a dim sum paradise, where traditional carts filled with steaming bamboo baskets offer an assortment of savory and sweet delicacies. Bite into fluffy char siu bao (barbecue pork buns), delicate har gow (shrimp dumplings), and custard-filled egg tarts that melt in your mouth.

- **Regional Specialties** – Beyond the well-known Cantonese dishes, Chinatown also offers regional specialties from various parts of China. Savor spicy Szechuan cuisine with dishes like mapo tofu and dan-dan noodles, or indulge in Shanghainese soup dumplings known as xiao long bao.

- **Bubble Tea and More** – Chinatown is also a haven for bubble tea lovers, with numerous shops offering diverse flavors and toppings to suit every palate.

- **Food Festivals** – Throughout the year, Chinatown hosts vibrant food festivals celebrating Chinese holidays, offering an opportunity to indulge in seasonal delights and experience the lively spirit of the community.

Little Italy

Photo by Louis Colbee from Unsplash

- **Italian Trattorias** – Little Italy, nestled in Manhattan, is a haven for lovers of Italian cuisine, boasting a charming ambiance reminiscent of the Old World. The neighborhood is home to classic trattorias, where you can enjoy rustic Italian dishes in a warm and inviting setting.

- **Pasta Dishes** – From al dente spaghetti to creamy fettuccine Alfredo, Little Italy's pasta offerings celebrate Italy's culinary prowess. Don't miss out on hearty dishes like lasagna and comforting risotto, served with various savory sauces.

- **Traditional Pastries** – Little Italy is renowned for its traditional Italian pastries and desserts. Indulge in cannoli filled with sweet ricotta, sfogliatelle with its delicate layers, and tiramisu that captures the essence of Italy in each spoonful.

- **Italian Gelato** – Beat the New York heat with a refreshing scoop of Italian gelato, with flavors ranging from classic pistachio and chocolate to inventive fruit combinations.

- **Food Events** – Little Italy hosts several food festivals throughout the year, including the Feast of San Gennaro, where you can savor a wide range of Italian treats while enjoying live music and cultural performances.

Koreatown

Photo by chensiyuan

- **Korean BBQ** – Koreatown, centered around West 32nd Street in Manhattan, is a carnivore's delight, offering traditional Korean BBQ restaurants where you can grill tender meats at your table. Don't forget to try samgyeopsal (pork belly), galbi (marinated beef short ribs), and bulgogi (marinated beef) for an unforgettable experience.

- **Hot Pot Delights** – Warm up during colder months with a hearty Korean hot pot, jeongol, or jjigae, brimming with fresh vegetables, meats, and flavorful broths.

- **Trendy Dessert Spots** – Koreatown is a paradise for dessert lovers, with trendy spots offering Instagram-worthy desserts like bingsu (shaved ice with toppings), Korean pancakes, and sweet rice cakes.

- **Korean Fried Chicken** – Craving crispy and flavorful fried chicken? Koreatown is home to several establishments serving Korean-style fried chicken, available in various sauces and levels of spiciness.

- **Karaoke and Late-Night Fun** – Beyond its culinary offerings, Koreatown comes alive at night with karaoke bars and lively late-night eateries, perfect for a memorable and fun-filled evening.

Trendy Dining Experiences

New York City is known for its dynamic and ever-evolving food scene, and trendy dining experiences have become a staple for food enthusiasts seeking innovative and unique culinary adventures. In this section, we'll uncover three trendy dining experiences that have captured the hearts of both locals and visitors.

Farm-to-Table Restaurants

Photo by Dan Gold from Unsplash

- **Sustainable Dining Options** – Farm-to-table restaurants focus on sourcing their ingredients directly from local farmers and producers, promoting sustainability and reducing the carbon footprint of their dishes. These establishments prioritize organic and ethically-sourced ingredients, ensuring a fresh and environmentally-friendly dining experience.

- **Seasonal Menus** – Farm-to-table restaurants embrace the changing seasons, adapting their menus accordingly to showcase the freshest and most flavorful ingredients available. Each visit to these establishments offers a new culinary journey that celebrates the bounties of nature.

- **Farm-Fresh Ingredients** – One of the highlights of dining at farm-to-table restaurants is the exceptional quality of the ingredients used in their dishes. Every plate reflects the passion and care invested in supporting local farmers, from vibrant vegetables to locally-raised meats.

- **Chef-Driven Creativity** – Chefs at farm-to-table restaurants often take inspiration from the seasonal produce and ingredients, resulting in innovative and delightful flavor combinations that celebrate the essence of the ingredients.

- **Connection to the Source** – Farm-to-table dining provides a unique opportunity for diners to connect with the origins of their food, fostering a deeper appreciation for the local food ecosystem.

Rooftop Bars and Restaurants

Photo by Alex Proimos

- **Panoramic Views** – Rooftop dining in New York City offers breathtaking views of the iconic skyline, making the dining experience truly unforgettable. Whether you're sipping cocktails or indulging in a gourmet meal, the backdrop of the city's towering skyscrapers creates a mesmerizing ambiance.

- **Craft Cocktails** – Rooftop bars are known for their creative and artisanal cocktail offerings, featuring unique combinations and fresh ingredients that tantalize the taste buds. Enjoying a craft cocktail against the backdrop of the city lights adds a touch of sophistication to any evening.

- **Trendy Ambiance** – Rooftop venues often boast stylish décor, providing a trendy and upscale setting for socializing and enjoying delectable cuisine.

- **Outdoor Oasis** – Amid the bustling city, rooftop bars and restaurants offer tranquility and escape, providing an ideal space to unwind and savor the moment.

- **Daytime and Nighttime Experiences** – Rooftop dining is just as enchanting during the day as at night. Whether seeking a sunny brunch or a romantic dinner under the stars, rooftop venues cater to various dining preferences.

Food Markets and Halls

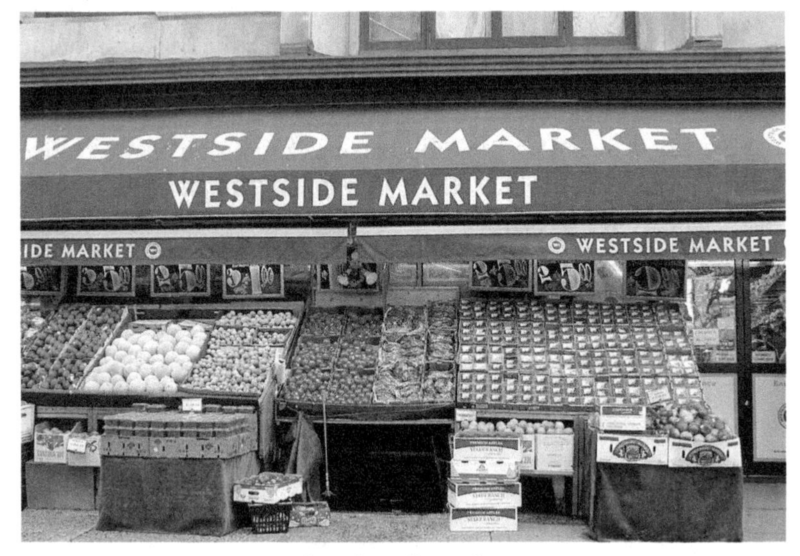

Photo by Billy Hathorn

- **Vibrant Food Markets** – Food markets in New York City, such as Chelsea Market and Smorgasburg, are lively and diverse hubs showcasing a wide array of culinary delights worldwide. These markets are a treasure trove for foodies seeking innovative dishes and unique flavors.

- **Diverse Vendors** – Food markets and halls host diverse food vendors representing various cuisines and cultural backgrounds. From gourmet eateries to street food stalls, there's something to please every palate.

- **Culinary Events** – Food markets often host special events, including tastings, cooking demonstrations, and pop-up experiences, where visitors can immerse themselves in the city's culinary culture.

- **Community Gathering Spaces** – Food markets and halls serve as vibrant community spaces, attracting locals and tourists to celebrate food, culture, and creativity.

- **Hidden Culinary Gems** – Exploring food markets unveils hidden culinary gems that may not be as well-known as established restaurants but offer equally delightful dining experiences.

In this chapter, we've delved into the trendiest dining experiences that New York City has to offer, from sustainable farm-to-table restaurants to elevated rooftop bars and vibrant food markets. Each experience celebrates the city's food passion and ever-evolving culinary landscape.

But the journey doesn't end here. The next chapter will take us off the beaten path, exploring hidden gems and lesser-known locations waiting to be discovered.

So, please put on your adventurous spirit, and let's venture into the lesser-explored corners of New York City's culinary wonders. Bon appétit!

CHAPTER 7

Hidden Gems and Off-the-Beaten-Path

Photo by Jakob Owens from Unsplash

Amidst the bustling streets and iconic landmarks of New York City lies a world of secrets waiting to be discovered—a treasure trove of hidden gems and off-the-beaten-path wonders that add a touch of mystery and enchantment to the city's charm. As you wander through the urban jungle, you may stumble upon a lesser-known attraction that captures your imagination and leaves you with unforgettable memories.

Let me take you on a journey with a captivating story about one such hidden gem tucked away in the heart of the city. Imagine strolling down a quiet side street, surrounded by the city's energy, when you spot an unassuming door between two grand buildings. Curiosity beckons, and you step inside, unsure of what awaits you beyond that threshold.

To your delight, you find yourself in a whimsical speakeasy, "The Enchanted Hourglass," a haven that seems plucked from the pages of a fairytale. Crystal chandeliers glow warmly, and a gentle melody fills the air. Bartenders, dressed in dapper attire, greet you with a friendly smile as they craft artful cocktails infused with flavors you've never encountered. Each sip is a revelation, an elixir that transports you to a world of wonder and delight.

As you chat with fellow patrons, you learn that "The Enchanted Hourglass" is known only to those who seek it out, a cherished secret among those who value unique experiences. Its ever-changing menu features rare spirits and exotic ingredients from far-flung corners, captivating seasoned connoisseurs and curious adventurers alike.

But "The Enchanted Hourglass" is just one of the many hidden gems that await your discovery in the intricate tapestry of New York City. Beyond the tourist trails and well-trodden paths are tucked-away treasures, lesser-known attractions, and cultural gems that will unveil a side of the city you never knew existed.

In this chapter, we'll embark on a voyage of exploration, seeking out the hidden gems and off-the-beaten-path locations that offer a glimpse into the city's best-kept secrets. From secret gardens to underground art galleries and tucked-away eateries to unconventional museums, we'll uncover the lesser-known side of New York City that will leave you enchanted and inspired.

So, let's step off the beaten path together and venture into New York's hidden wonders. The city awaits, ready to unveil its best-kept secrets, and all you need to do is take that first step into the unknown.

Unique Attractions

New York City's allure lies in its iconic landmarks and hidden treasures—unique attractions that reveal a different side of the city's character. In this section, we'll venture off the beaten path to discover some of New York's most intriguing and lesser-known wonders that charm the urban landscape.

High Line Park

Photo by Dana Andreea Gheorghe from Unsplash

- **Elevated Green Space** – High Line Park, a marvel of urban design, transforms an old railway line into a stunning elevated green space, providing a serene oasis above the bustling streets. The park stretches through Manhattan's Chelsea neighborhood, offering a peaceful escape with vibrant gardens and lush vegetation.

- **Urban Design and Architecture** – High Line Park's design ingeniously incorporates remnants of the historic railway, including vintage tracks and original railings, blending industrial elements with modern aesthetics. The elevated pathway grants visitors a unique perspective of the city as they meander above streets and intersections.

- **Art Installations** - The park frequently hosts captivating art installations, adding an artistic touch to the urban environment. Visitors can encounter sculptures, murals, and interactive exhibits that enhance the park's creative ambiance.

- **Seasonal Beauty** - High Line Park's beauty changes with the seasons, delighting visitors with a blooming spring, a lush summer, colorful autumn, and a serene winter landscape. Each visit offers a different sensory experience as nature evolves throughout the year.

- **Community Events** - Beyond its scenic charm, High Line Park hosts various community events, including cultural festivals, outdoor performances, and educational programs, fostering a sense of unity among locals and visitors.

Roosevelt Island Tramway

Photo by Jim.henderson

- **Aerial Tram Experience** – The Roosevelt Island Tramway, an aerial cable car system, connects Manhattan's Upper East Side to Roosevelt Island, providing a thrilling and picturesque mode of transportation. As you soar above the East River, you'll be treated to breathtaking views of the Manhattan skyline and the Queensboro Bridge.

- **Stunning Views** – The tramway offers a panoramic vista of New York City's iconic landmarks, from the Empire State Building to the United Nations Headquarters. Sunset rides are particularly enchanting, casting the city in a golden glow.

- **Island Exploration** – Once on Roosevelt Island, visitors can explore the island's peaceful ambiance, dotted with scenic waterfront promenades and scenic parks. Don't miss the tranquil beauty of Four Freedoms Park, dedicated to President Franklin D. Roosevelt.

- **The Octagon: A Hidden Gem** – The historic Octagon building, formerly part of the New York City Lunatic Asylum, stands as a captivating architectural gem on Roosevelt Island. Today, it houses residential units and a unique cultural space.

- **Escape from the City Bustle** – The Roosevelt Island Tramway offers a brief respite from the city's hustle and bustle, providing a calm and relaxing journey that makes you feel worlds away from Manhattan's busy streets.

Grand Central Terminal Whispering Gallery

Photo by Stephen H from Unsplash

- **Acoustic Phenomenon** – One of Grand Central Terminal's most intriguing features is the Whispering Gallery outside the famous Oyster Bar & Restaurant. Stand in diagonal corners of the gallery, whisper, and your words will travel across the curved ceiling, allowing someone on the other side to hear as if you were next to them.

- **Secrets of the Whispering Arch** – The phenomenon results from the gallery's curved architecture, which creates a perfect parabolic sound reflection. The unique design was intended to allow architects to communicate easily, but it became a delightful surprise for visitors.

- **Other Hidden Features** – Grand Central Terminal is home to other hidden gems, such as the celestial mural on the main concourse's ceiling, depicting the constellations in reverse order.

- **Vanderbilt Hall** – Vanderbilt Hall, a majestic space within the terminal, frequently hosts art exhibitions, events, and pop-up shops, adding to the terminal's vibrant atmosphere.

- **History and Timelessness** – Beyond its practical function, Grand Central Terminal stands as an architectural marvel and a testament to New York's rich history, making it more than just a transportation hub—it's a destination.

Quirky Museums and Sights

In a city as diverse and vibrant as New York, it's no surprise that some museums and sights defy convention and offer a unique twist on art, history, and culture. This section explores some of the quirkiest and most intriguing destinations that will leave you marveling at the city's boundless creativity and eccentricity.

Mmuseumm

Photo by Alexkalman

- **Unconventional Exhibitions** – Mmuseumm is a tiny museum with a big impact, occupying an elevator shaft in a converted freight elevator in Tribeca. Its unconventional exhibitions challenge traditional museum norms, offering an intimate and immersive experience.

- **Curated Oddities** – Mmuseumm's curators have a knack for selecting seemingly mundane objects and transforming them into thought-provoking displays. Each piece tells a fascinating and unexpected story, from everyday items to cultural artifacts.

- **Thought-Provoking Displays** - The museum's thought-provoking exhibits often prompt visitors to question societal norms and ponder the meaning of ordinary objects. It's a place where the mundane becomes extraordinary.

- **Intimate Setting** - The small space of Mmuseumm fosters an intimate connection between the exhibits and the visitors, encouraging contemplation and engagement.

- **Hidden Gem** - Mmuseumm's unassuming location and inconspicuous entrance make it a true hidden gem, known mainly to those seeking unconventional museum experiences.

The Cloisters

Photo by GK tramrunner RU

- **Medieval Art and Architecture** - The Cloisters in Fort Tryon Park is an extension of The Metropolitan Museum of Art devoted to medieval European art and architecture. The museum's tranquil setting and architectural elements evoke the atmosphere of a European monastery.

- **Serene Museum Experience** - The Cloisters' serene ambiance offers a peaceful retreat from the city's hustle and bustle, providing visitors with a calming and immersive art experience.

- **Remarkable Collections** - The museum's collections include exquisite medieval artworks such as illuminated manuscripts, sculptures, stained glass windows, and tapestries. Each piece is a testament to the craftsmanship and artistic brilliance of the medieval era.

- **Gardens and Courtyards** - The Cloisters' beautifully landscaped gardens and courtyards further enhance the medieval ambiance, creating a picturesque setting for contemplation and reflection.

- **Architectural Gems** - The museum's architectural features, including its Romanesque and Gothic elements, make it an architectural gem in its own right, transporting visitors to a bygone era.

Federal Hall National Memorial

Photo by Bjoertvedt

- **Historical Significance** – Federal Hall National Memorial, located on Wall Street, holds tremendous historical significance as the site of George Washington's presidential inauguration in 1789. It was also the first capitol building in the United States and served as a meeting place for Congress.

- **Exhibits and Artifacts** – The memorial houses exhibits and artifacts highlighting key moments in early American history, including the formation of the U.S. Constitution and the Bill of Rights.

- **Connection to the Founding of the United States** – Standing on the same ground where the founding fathers once stood, visitors can sense the weight of history and the ideals that shaped the nation.

- **Iconic Wall Street Location** – Federal Hall's location in the heart of Wall Street adds to its allure, making it an easily accessible destination for history enthusiasts and curious travelers.

- **Symbol of Democracy** – As a national memorial, Federal Hall stands as a symbol of the country's democratic principles and a reminder of the enduring legacy of the American Revolution.

Neighborhood Secrets

Beyond the famous landmarks, New York City is a patchwork of neighborhoods with distinct characters and hidden treasures. In this section, we'll venture off the tourist track and uncover the neighborhood secrets that offer a glimpse into the city's authentic charm and local culture.

Village Speakeasies

- **Hidden Bars and Speakeasy Culture** – The East Village is known for its speakeasy culture, where hidden bars pay homage to the city's Prohibition-era history. Discover secret entrances concealed behind bookshelves, phone booths, and unmarked doors.

- **Craft Cocktails and Intimate Ambiance** – Speakeasies in the East Village boast expert mixologists who create craft cocktails with precision and flair. The intimate ambiance and dimly lit interiors transport you back to an era of clandestine revelry.

- **Unique Themes and Settings** – Each speakeasy has its unique theme and setting, ranging from retro-inspired lounges to moody jazz dens. Expect surprises around every corner as these hidden gems blend innovation with vintage charm.

- **Reservation Secrets** – Some speakeasies require reservations or secret codes for entry, adding an element of exclusivity and intrigue to the experience.

- **Insider's Guide** – Locals in the East Village hold the keys to the best-hidden bars, making discussing and discovering the neighborhood's best-kept secrets worthwhile.

Brooklyn Heights Promenade

Photo by Beyond My Ken

- **Stunning Views of the Manhattan Skyline** – The Brooklyn Heights Promenade, a picturesque esplanade along the East River, offers postcard-worthy views of the Manhattan skyline. It's a favorite spot for locals and visitors to capture breathtaking photographs.

- **Historic Architecture** – Stroll through the charming streets of Brooklyn Heights, lined with historic brownstones and elegant townhouses. The neighborhood's architectural splendor is a testament to its rich history and timeless beauty.

- **Tranquil and Scenic Retreat** – The promenade's tranquil setting provides a welcome escape from the city's fast-paced energy, offering a serene space for relaxation and contemplation.

- **Brooklyn Bridge Access** – The promenade conveniently connects to the iconic Brooklyn Bridge, allowing visitors to embark on a scenic walk across the river to Manhattan.

- **Cafés and Parks** – After enjoying the views, explore the nearby cafés and parks that dot the neighborhood, adding to the laid-back charm of Brooklyn Heights.

Governors Island

Photo by Laura Peruchi from Unsplash

- **Peaceful Atmosphere** – Governors Island, a short ferry ride from Manhattan, provides a peaceful retreat away from the city's crowds and noise. The island's car-free policy contributes to its serene ambiance.

- **Bike Rentals** – The best way to explore Governors Island is by renting a bike, allowing you to cycle leisurely around the island's expansive green spaces and historic sites.

- **Seasonal Events and Activities** – Governors Island hosts various seasonal events, including art installations, concerts, and festivals, making each visit a unique experience.

- **Historic Landmarks** – The island is home to several historic landmarks, including Fort Jay and Castle Williams, offering a glimpse into the island's military past.

- **Picnic Spots and Hammock Groves** – Take a break and relax in the island's picnic spots and hammock groves, where you can enjoy a leisurely afternoon with views of the Statue of Liberty and the Manhattan skyline.

In this chapter, we've unveiled the quirky museums and sights that add an unconventional twist to New York's cultural landscape. From the unconventional exhibits of Mmuseumm to the medieval charm of The Cloisters and the historical significance of the Federal Hall National Memorial, each destination offers a unique perspective on the city's history, creativity, and eccentricity.

But the exploration doesn't end here. The next chapter will take us on day trips from New York, where we'll venture beyond the city's boundaries and discover the captivating destinations that lie just a stone's throw away. So, let's step off the tourist track and continue our journey into the hidden gems and neighborhood secrets that make New York City a treasure trove of discovery.

CHAPTER 8

Day Trips from New York

Photo by Amels from Unsplash

Picture this: the sun rises over the iconic New York City skyline, casting a golden glow on the towering skyscrapers. As the city awakens with its characteristic energy, you embark on an adventure beyond its boundaries. This day trip promises new experiences, breathtaking sights, and the allure of the unknown.

One early morning, I set out on my day trip from New York City, craving a change of scenery and the chance to explore the hidden gems lying just beyond the city's reach. The anticipation filled the air as my friends, and I hopped on a train, eager to uncover the delights that awaited us in the surrounding landscapes.

Our destination? A quaint coastal town with a rich maritime history, where the aroma of saltwater mingled with the scent of freshly baked pastries. The old-fashioned charm of the streets was like a step back in time, and we found ourselves enchanted by the friendly locals and the warm embrace of the community.

We wandered along the waterfront, the sea breeze on our faces, and discovered a hidden beach nestled between rugged cliffs and adorned with seashells glistening in the sand. With the city's hum now a distant memory, we reveled in the tranquility of the ocean's rhythm and felt a sense of serenity wash over us.

Later in the day, we explored a nearby nature reserve, immersing ourselves in the lush greenery and the soothing sound of birdsong. It was a welcome escape from the concrete jungle, a chance to reconnect with nature's beauty and rediscover the joy of simply being present at the moment.

As the sun descended, we savored a seafood feast at a local restaurant—plates brimming with fresh catches from the nearby fishing boats. The flavors danced on our tongues, a testament to the region's culinary traditions and the passion of its chefs.

As the day drew close, we sat by the harbor, watching the sun's fiery hues blend with the waters, painting the sky in a mesmerizing canvas of colors. The moment's beauty etched itself in our hearts, a memory that would forever remain a cherished part of our New York experience.

This day trip reminded us of the wonders that await beyond the city's borders—a world of exploration, beauty, and unexpected treasures. In this chapter, we'll embark on a series of day trips from New York City, each offering its distinct allure and promising a journey of discovery. The endless possibilities and adventures are boundless, from charming towns and scenic landscapes to historical sites and cultural escapes. So, let's set forth and explore the captivating destinations that lie just a short trip away from the heart of the city.

Hudson Valley

Nestled north of New York City, the Hudson Valley beckons with its picturesque landscapes, rich history, and cultural allure. This region, renowned for its scenic beauty and artistic treasures, offers a perfect escape for day-trippers seeking a blend of nature, art, and history. Let's venture into the Hudson Valley and explore its fascinating destinations.

Storm King Art Center

Photo by MJ

- **Outdoor Sculptures** – Storm King Art Center boasts an extraordinary collection of large-scale outdoor sculptures amidst rolling hills and meadows. The sculptures, crafted by prominent artists, harmoniously blend with the natural landscape, creating a captivating open-air gallery.

- **Beautiful Landscapes** – The center's 500-acre landscape serves as a stunning backdrop for the art installations, offering visitors a chance to immerse themselves in nature's beauty.

- **Seasonal Exhibitions** – Storm King Art Center hosts seasonal exhibitions introducing new artworks and installations, inviting visitors to experience the ever-changing art landscape.

- **Art and Environment** – The center's commitment to environmental stewardship enhances the connection between art and nature, creating a unique and sustainable art experience.

- **Family-Friendly Activities** – Families visiting Storm King can participate in engaging art programs and interactive experiences designed to inspire creativity and curiosity in children.

Sleepy Hollow

Photo by Bestbudbrian

- **Literary Connections** – Sleepy Hollow, made famous by Washington Irving's classic tale "The Legend of Sleepy Hollow," invites visitors to enter the world of Ichabod Crane and the Headless Horseman. The town's historic sites and landmarks evoke the spirit of Irving's timeless story.

- **Haunted History** – Ghost tours and attractions make Sleepy Hollow a must-visit destination for those seeking spine-chilling thrills and a taste of the supernatural.

- **Scenic Beauty** – Sleepy Hollow's setting along the Hudson River provides a tranquil escape, with picturesque vistas and scenic spots perfect for strolls.

- **Historic Cemeteries** – Explore the town's historic cemeteries, including the Sleepy Hollow Cemetery, where Washington Irving's final resting place lies beneath a majestic monument.

- **Fall Foliage** – In the fall, Sleepy Hollow's landscape transforms into a colorful tapestry, attracting visitors to witness the breathtaking beauty of autumn in the Hudson Valley.

West Point Military Academy

Photo by Dave Lowe from Unsplash

- **Guided Tours** – West Point Military Academy offers guided tours that provide insight into the academy's history, traditions, and cadet life. Visitors can learn about the rigorous training and education that shapes the future leaders of the U.S. Army.

- **Military History** – The academy's rich military history is showcased in its museums, featuring exhibits on the American Revolution, the Civil War, and other significant periods.

- **Panoramic Views of the Hudson River** – West Point's strategic location on a bluff overlooking the Hudson River offers visitors stunning vistas of the river and its surroundings.

- **Historic Buildings** – The campus is adorned with historic buildings, including the iconic Cadet Chapel and the Trophy Point Amphitheater, where concerts and events occur.

- **Honor and Tradition** – Visiting West Point offers an opportunity to witness the academy's commitment to honor, discipline, and the development of future leaders in the U.S. military.

The Hamptons

The Hamptons, a collection of charming towns on the eastern end of Long Island, have long been synonymous with luxury, leisure, and artistic sophistication. Offering a retreat for the affluent and the artistic alike, the Hamptons lure visitors with their pristine beaches, cultural attractions, and vibrant social scene. Let's venture into the Hamptons and experience their unique coastal charm.

East Hampton

Photo by Calvin Uy from Unsplash

- **Pristine Beaches** – East Hampton's coastline is adorned with pristine beaches, where sunbathing, beachcombing, and water activities beckon. Main Beach, known for its scenic beauty, attracts locals and visitors alike.

- **Upscale Shopping** – The town's charming streets are lined with upscale boutiques, galleries, and designer shops, catering to discerning shoppers.

- **Art Galleries** - East Hampton's art scene flourishes with numerous galleries showcasing works by established and emerging artists. Art enthusiasts will find a wealth of creative expressions to explore.

- **Historic Landmarks** - The town has several historic landmarks, including the Mulford Farm Museum and the Home Sweet Home Museum, which offer a glimpse into the region's past.

- **Culinary Delights** - East Hampton's dining scene offers a delightful range of restaurants, from fine dining establishments to casual seafood shacks, satisfying every culinary craving.

Montauk

Photo by Bernd Dittrich from Unsplash

- **Lighthouses** - Montauk is home to the iconic Montauk Point Lighthouse, New York State's oldest lighthouse. Visitors can climb to the top for panoramic views of the Atlantic Ocean and Block Island Sound.

- **Surfing Spots** - Known as the "Surfing Capital of the East Coast," Montauk's beaches attract surfers seeking the region's best waves. Lessons and surfboard rentals are available for those new to the sport.

- **Fresh Seafood Eateries** – Montauk's fishing heritage is celebrated in its numerous seafood restaurants, serving freshly caught fish and delectable shellfish.

- **Hiking and Nature Trails** – Nature enthusiasts can explore the area's scenic beauty through hiking trails, such as the Montauk Point Trail and the Hither Hills State Park trail system.

- **Montauk Downs State Park** – Golf enthusiasts can tee off at the picturesque Montauk Downs State Park, a championship 18-hole golf course surrounded by stunning landscapes.

Sag Harbor

Photo by Max Harlynking from Unsplash

- **Charming Harbor** – Sag Harbor's historic whaling port boasts a picturesque harbor lined with sailboats and yachts, exuding maritime charm.

- **Historic Homes** – The town's streets are graced with well-preserved historic homes, reflecting its colonial past and architectural diversity.

- **Cultural Attractions** – Sag Harbor is a hub of cultural activity, with theaters, galleries, and music venues offering a rich tapestry of artistic experiences.

- **Long Wharf** – Long Wharf, extending into the harbor, provides a scenic spot for strolling, picnicking, and watching the sunset.

- **Boutique Shopping** – Sag Harbor's boutiques and specialty shops offer unique finds, from artisanal crafts to fashionable clothing, making it a shopper's delight.

Fire Island

Fire Island is a captivating barrier island located just off the southern coast of Long Island, New York. This narrow strip stretches for 32 miles and offers a breathtaking blend of pristine beaches, diverse ecosystems, and vibrant communities. Fire Island is a cherished destination for beach lovers, nature enthusiasts, and those seeking a relaxed escape from the bustling city.

With its unique charm, LGBTQ+-friendly atmosphere, and outdoor activities, Fire Island promises an unforgettable retreat in the heart of nature's beauty.

Robert Moses State Park

Photo by Jueun Song from Unsplash

- **Beautiful Beaches** – Robert Moses State Park on Fire Island offers some of Long Island's most beautiful beaches, attracting sun-seekers and lovers. Its soft sands and rolling waves provide an ideal setting for relaxation and recreation.

- **Nature Trails** – The park features nature trails that lead through dunes and marshlands, allowing visitors to explore the island's diverse ecosystems.

- **Opportunities for Outdoor Activities** – Robert Moses State Park provides ample outdoor activities such as fishing, birdwatching, and picnicking.

- **Lighthouse** – The park is home to the Fire Island Lighthouse, where visitors can climb to the top for stunning views of the Atlantic Ocean and the bay.

- **Family-Friendly Amenities** – The park offers family-friendly amenities, including playgrounds, bathhouses, and concession stands, making it a popular destination for all ages.

Cherry Grove

Photo by Bernd Dittrich

Fire Island's Cherry Grove is a beautiful coastal destination and a vibrant LGBTQ+ community that embraces diversity and celebrates inclusivity. This subsection invites you to explore Cherry Grove's unique charm and welcoming atmosphere.

- **LGBTQ+ Community** - Cherry Grove is known for its strong LGBTQ+ community, providing a safe and inclusive space for everyone to be themselves—the Grove's reputation as a welcoming haven dates back to the 1940s.

- **Vibrant Nightlife** - Cherry Grove comes alive at night with its vibrant nightlife, featuring drag shows, dance parties, and beachside bonfires. Visitors can expect a fun-filled and energetic social scene.

- **Beach Culture** - Acceptance, body positivity, and a carefree spirit mark the beach culture in Cherry Grove. The shore becomes a lively gathering spot where friends gather to bask in the sun and enjoy each other's company.

- **Creative Expression** - The artistic spirit of Cherry Grove is evident in its many events, including art shows, performances, and community theater productions.

- **Cherished Memories** - Many visitors to Cherry Grove return year after year, creating lasting memories and forging strong connections with the community.

Sunken Forest

- **Unique Ecosystem** - Sunken Forest is a rare maritime holly forest nestled between dunes and the bay, offering a distinct ecosystem with diverse flora and fauna.

- **Guided Nature Walks** - Visitors can join guided nature walks led by experts who share insights into the forest's ecological significance.

- **Birdwatching Opportunities** - Sunken Forest is a haven for birdwatchers, with various bird species frequenting the area. Binoculars in hand, you may spot colorful warblers, majestic herons, and graceful egrets.

- **Botanical Marvels** - The forest's unique environment nurtures remarkable plant life, including delicate orchids, gnarled cedars, and resilient beach heather.

- **Peaceful Retreat** - As you meander along the forest's boardwalks, you'll be enveloped in tranquility, with the only sounds being the rustle of leaves and the occasional call of a bird.

As we conclude our exploration of the day trips from New York City, we've uncovered the beauty and diversity that lie just beyond the city's hustle and bustle. From the artistic allure of the Hudson Valley to the coastal charm of the Hamptons and the natural wonders of Fire Island, each destination has left its mark on our journey of discovery.

But our exploration doesn't end here. The next chapter will whisk us away on longer excursions as we embark on unforgettable adventures beyond the city's borders. So, let's pack our bags, fuel our wanderlust, and continue our exploration of the hidden gems and captivating destinations that await us in the world beyond New York City.

CONCLUSION

Photo by Ramil Ugot from Pexels

As we reach the end of this journey through the vibrant streets, iconic landmarks, and hidden gems of New York City, it is evident that this city has a magical way of leaving an indelible mark on our souls. Exploring the Big Apple is not just an adventure; it's a transformative experience that touches our hearts and broadens our perspectives in ways we never imagined.

From Times Square's bustling energy to Central Park's serenity, each corner of the city holds a unique story, a memory waiting to be cherished. We've ventured into the past at historical landmarks, danced to the rhythm of diverse cultures, and indulged in culinary delights that awakened our taste buds. Through museums and galleries, we've witnessed the depth of human creativity, while the vibrant street art reminded us of the power of self-expression.

But perhaps the most transformative aspect of New York City is the people who call it home and the visitors who become a part of its vibrant tapestry. The city's diversity embraces us with open arms, breaking down barriers and fostering connections that transcend boundaries. In shared laughter, random encounters with strangers, and a profound sense of belonging, we discover the true essence of New York's spirit.

As we say goodbye to the towering skyscrapers and iconic landmarks, we carry the memories of sunsets over the Hudson River, the echoes of music from jazz clubs, the beauty of blossoming cherry trees in spring, and the laughter of children in the city parks. New York City has imprinted on our hearts, forever changing how we see the world and reminding us that adventure lies around every corner, whether in the heart of a bustling metropolis or a quaint neighborhood.

May the transformative experience of exploring New York City inspire us to embrace the spirit of curiosity and wanderlust in all aspects of life. Just as this city has unveiled its treasures, may we continue to seek the hidden gems and off-the-beaten-path destinations that await us in our future travels.

As we bid farewell to the pages of this book, let us carry the spirit of New York City within us—a spirit of resilience, creativity, and boundless possibility. Whether we return to its vibrant streets or venture to new horizons, may the magic of New York always remind us that every adventure, big or small, can transform us in the most extraordinary ways. So let's step forward, eager to explore the world, for the journey never truly ends—it simply evolves, as do we.

Made in the USA
Coppell, TX
13 April 2024